Project 2027

Project 2027

A Bold Plan for Democrats to Pass Laws that Improve the Quality of Life, Advance Democracy, and Win Elections

Ed Minnock
Published by Ed Minnock & Associates

Copyright © 2025 by Ed Minnock

Version 4.0

All rights reserved. No part of this book may be reproduced in any form or by any electronic or mechanical means, including information storage and retrieval systems, without written permission from the author, except in the case of a reviewer, who may quote brief passages embodied in critical articles or in a review.

Trademarked names may appear throughout this book. Rather than use a trademark symbol with every occurrence of a trademarked name, names are used editorially, with no intention of infringement of the respective owner's trademark.

The information in this book is distributed on an "as is" basis, without warranty. Although every precaution has been taken in the preparation of this work, neither the author nor the publisher shall have any liability to any person or entity concerning any loss or damage caused or alleged to be caused directly or indirectly by the information contained in this book.

Cover design by Crisley Thome.

All rights reserved.

ISBN: 979-8-9989690-0-3

Dedication

For Jody and Killy, also Tom, Bill, Joan, and John

Contents

Dedication 5

Introduction 9

Women Are People, Corporations Are Not 12

Better Health Through Affordable Healthcare 36

Affordable Housing 51

Raise Minimum Wage 59

Advance Democracy 67

Project 2027 New Rules 79

2029 and Beyond 88

The Colorado Way 91

About the Author 95

Bibliography 97

End Notes 99

Introduction

The 2024 federal elections did not go well for the Democrats. Trump was reelected president, and the Republicans won both houses of Congress. The Republicans also hold a six-to-three majority on the Supreme Court. This book does not dwell on what happened. Instead, it provides a blueprint for making Americans' lives better and winning elections.

America Has Challenges

Although America has the world's strongest economy and military, middle-class opportunities have declined while the cost of housing and healthcare has skyrocketed. These trends have caused the quality of life to deteriorate for millions of Americans. As a result, America leads the developed world in inequality, poverty rate, incarceration rate, suicide rate, drug overdose rate, gun violence, obesity, healthcare costs, and the number of homeless people (France has a higher percentage of homeless). America is last in the developed world in terms of life expectancy.[1][2][3][4]

Introduction

Further, a 2020 study of 163 countries revealed that the U.S. was one of only three countries whose quality of life declined during the previous decade, and the U.S. declined the most.[5]

Worse, Americans are angry at each other. Roughly 70 percent of both Republicans and Democrats claim the other party is "a serious threat to the United States and its people."[6]

However, there are many important policy issues that Americans overwhelmingly agree upon:

1. Eighty-eight percent of Americans want big money out of politics.[7]
2. Eighty-three percent of Americans want the government to lower the prices of prescription drugs.[8]
3. Seventy-eight percent want Congress to address high housing costs.[9]
4. Seventy-eight percent support limiting hospitals' costs.[10]
5. Seventy-four percent say the federal minimum wage, currently $7.25 per hour, should be raised to $20 per hour.[11]
6. Seventy percent oppose immunity for the President of the United States.[12]
7. Seventy percent want the Supreme Court to stop gerrymandering.[13]
8. Sixty-five percent want the popular vote, not the electoral college, to decide who is President.[14]

Introduction

9. Sixty-three percent think Roe v. Wade should not have been overturned.[15]
10. Sixty-three percent support restoring the Voting Rights Act.[16]

These ten policies will improve the quality of life for most Americans and advance democracy. Further, all these policies can be implemented through moral, legal, and constitutional means without any amendments and without raising taxes.

This book recommends that Democrats campaign in the 2026 midterms on a quality-of-life platform that commits to passing bills that implement the policies listed above. If President Trump vetoes the bills, he can be exposed for opposing popular legislation that makes life better for Americans. Democrats can then promise to pass the legislation again when a Democrat sits in the Oval Office.

This book predicts that this quality-of-life platform will secure both houses of Congress in 2026 and win the Presidency while retaining both houses of Congress in 2028. The following chapters explain how.

Chapter 1

Women Are People, Corporations Are Not

Two of the Supreme Court's least popular decisions are *Dobbs v. Jackson Women's Health Organization,* which overturned *Roe v. Wade,* and *Citizens United v. Federal Election Commission,* which allows corporations to spend unlimited amounts of money on elections. In these rulings, the Court decided that women do not have a right to reproductive freedom, but corporations do have a right to free speech, and money is speech.[17][18]

With *Citizens United,* corporations added free speech to their list of rights that already included freedom of religion, Fourth Amendment privacy rights, due process, equal protection, and property rights, along with limited liability, perpetual life, and no chance of prison or house arrest. Of course, corporations cannot become pregnant. In several states, women face felony convictions and the threat of prison for ending unwanted pregnancies.[19]

To reach these decisions, the Supreme Court cited its understanding of the Constitution and the Amendments. However, neither corporations nor women's reproductive rights are mentioned in the Constitution or the Amendments. Further, both rulings reversed previous Supreme Court decisions with justifications that were at best controversial.[20] [21] If it appears that there is a flaw in America's legal system, there is.

Article I, Section 1 of the Constitution grants all legislative power to Congress. This chapter explains how Congress can use its constitutional powers to enact legislation that carries out the will of the people and improves the quality of life for Americans.

Supreme Court Takes Away Women's Rights

On June 24, 2022, the Supreme Court used its *Dobbs* ruling to overturn *Roe v. Wade*. Never had the Court removed a fundamental right from so many people. The *Dobbs* ruling triggered several state laws outlawing abortion, some of which were passed before women had the right to vote.[22] The ruling was devastating for women in many states who had, for forty-nine years, been able to arrange their lives around an expectation of control over their reproductive health, including having access to abortion. In many states, women were forced to continue with unwanted pregnancies, which made it more difficult to fully participate in modern social and economic life. In 2025, twelve states had total bans on abortion, four states had bans after six weeks, and two had bans after twelve weeks.[23]

Before the *Dobbs* ruling, but after a draft was leaked, House Democrats passed the Women's Health Protection Act. A vote was held in the Senate, and the bill received just forty-nine votes, far below the sixty votes needed to overcome the filibuster.[24]

The conservative assault on women's rights is not over. Project 2025 states that the *Dobbs* decision is just the beginning, and "the next conservative President should work with Congress to enact more robust protections for the unborn."[25]

Let Voters Decide Women's Reproductive Rights

Few issues are as divisive and politically polarizing in America as women's right to choose. A primary reason is that courts, not elected representatives or voters, have made key decisions on this issue. In Italy and Ireland, two primarily catholic countries that allow referendums, women have been granted the right to choose without divisiveness and violence.[26] (A referendum is a proposal that originates from the government and is voted on by voters.)

In 2018, Ireland held a referendum to decide whether to repeal its near-total ban on abortion. The ban was repealed by a vote of 66.4 percent to 33.6 percent.[27] In 1978, Italy's parliament passed a law legalizing abortion, similar to *Roe v. Wade*. Italy's far-right groups attempted to repeal the law, while far-left groups sought to expand it, both through national referendums. Voters overwhelmingly rejected both efforts, allowing the law to stand and effectively settling the issue.[28]

However, in Wichita, Kansas, an abortion clinic was attacked in 1986 with a pipe bomb. In 1993, Dr. George Tiller, a well-known abortion doctor, was shot and injured. In 2009, Dr. Tiller was shot and killed at his Wichita church. However, after the *Dobbs* ruling, Kansas voters rejected a proposed state constitutional amendment that would have specified that the right to terminate a pregnancy is not protected. This time, citizens accepted the results because voters decided. Most states that outlaw women's reproductive rights have not put the issue to a vote.[29] These are examples of citizens being more accepting of policy decisions made by voters.

In America, holding binding national votes on policy would require an Amendment because the Constitution does not grant voters that right. However, amending the Constitution is nearly impossible because it requires 290 votes of the 435 members of the House of Representatives, sixty-seven votes of the 100 members of the Senate, plus thousands of votes in state legislatures to achieve the required thirty-eight-state ratification. A study of thirty-two national constitutions found that the U.S. Constitution is the most difficult to amend.[30]

Congress could, however, schedule advisory referendums. Congress and the President are not legally bound to implement advisory referendums. Still, Congress and/or the President could commit to passing bills that implement the will of the people if they choose.

> British Prime Minister David Cameron held an advisory referendum on EU membership, called Brexit, and he vowed to carry out the will of the people, which the UK government did. The Brexit advisory referendum required a simple majority to pass.[31]

To ensure overwhelming voter support, this book recommends that a two-thirds supermajority is needed to pass an advisory referendum. (Two-thirds is chosen because that is what amendments require of both houses of Congress.) Passing the two-thirds threshold is important because it will be used to justify the new rules described below. For comparison, Donald Trump was elected twice without receiving 50 percent of the vote, while Joe Biden obtained 51 percent in 2020.[32] [33]

Once in power in 2027, Congressional Democrats should draft a bill to restore the basic elements of *Roe v. Wade*. Democrats should not have trouble passing such a bill in the House of Representatives because a simple majority is required. However, according to Senate rules, Senators who oppose a bill can extend debate by using a filibuster and effectively block a bill. Sixty votes are required to end a filibuster. Unless Democrats have a sixty-vote Senate majority, there is a good chance that Senate Republicans would filibuster a bill that restores women's reproductive rights. In that event, this book recommends that Congressional Democrats draft a bill that schedules an advisory referendum to vote on restoring the basic elements of *Roe v. Wade,* and that Senate Democrats establish a new rule: bills scheduling advisory referendums are not subject to Senate filibusters. (Chapter 6 explains how to establish filibuster rules.)

In a 2023 poll, 63 percent of Americans believed *Roe* should not have been overturned. To strengthen the referendum, Democrats could add the right to purchase contraceptives and abortion pills because those rights are also under threat.

The president would then have three choices. He can sign the bill into law, veto it, or do nothing. If he does nothing, the bill becomes law after ten days, excluding Sundays, assuming Congress is in session.[34] If the President threatens to veto the bill, Democrats could remind him that a national vote on women's reproductive rights would clear up any confusion regarding where voters stand on the issue. If the President vetoes the bill, Democrats can promise to pass a law guaranteeing women's reproductive rights again when a Democrat sits in the Oval Office.

If the bill scheduling the referendum becomes law and the advisory referendum passes the two-thirds threshold, Democrats should draft a bill that restores women's reproductive rights and secures women's right to purchase contraceptives and abortion pills. Democrats should reach across the aisle and invite Republicans to vote for the bill because it carries out the will of the people. Again, Democrats should not have trouble passing such a bill in the House of

Representatives because a simple majority is required. However, because there is a good chance that Senate Republicans would filibuster this bill, this book recommends that Senate Democrats establish a second new rule: bills that have received two-thirds of the vote in an advisory referendum are not subjected to Senate filibusters.

In that event, Republicans will likely call it a power grab by the Democrats and a sad day for the Senate. Republicans, however, could be reminded that in 2017, Senate Republicans, led by Senate leader Mitch McConnell, ended the filibuster on Supreme Court justices to confirm Neil Gorsuch after blocking President Obama's nominee, Merrick Garland, for nine months. A simple majority was also used to confirm Brett Kavanaugh and fast-track Amy Coney Barrett. After securing Barrett's confirmation, McConnell bragged, "I certainly didn't expect to have three Supreme Court justices. At the risk of tooting my own horn, look at the majority leaders since L.B.J. and find another one who was able to do something as consequential as this."[35] Less than two years later, *Roe* was overturned.

Once passed, pressure would be on President Trump to sign the bill. If he vetoes it, he exposes himself for opposing legislation that voters overwhelmingly support, and the Democrats could promise to pass the legislation again when a Democrat sits in the Oval Office. Once signed into law, the Supreme Court would most likely let it stand because Congress has passed several laws that grant rights to citizens that the

Supreme Court has not overturned, such as the Civil Rights Act of 1964, the Americans with Disabilities Act, the Age Discrimination in Employment Act, and the Pregnancy Discrimination Act.[36]

However, if the Supreme Court were to strike down the law, Democrats in Congress might be able to draft and pass a new law that accommodates the Court's objections. If not, Democrats could consider invoking the Exceptions Clause.

Article III, Section 2, Clause 2 of the Constitution, called the Exceptions Clause, explicitly grants Congress the power to limit the Supreme Court's appellate jurisdiction, meaning Congress can decide which classes of cases the Supreme Court can hear and rule upon. Further, the text in the Exceptions Clause is clear and unambiguous, unlike other parts of the Constitution and the Amendments.[37]

However, because the Exceptions Clause has been rarely used, invoking it could trigger accusations of unfairness, resulting in a loss of public support. Consequently, the Exceptions Clause should only be used under very specific circumstances. This book recommends that Democrats establish a third new rule: the Exceptions Clause can be used under the following conditions: the law in question advances democracy (e.g. promotes human rights or the rule of law or eliminates corruption), the law does not conflict with what the Constitution and Amendments explicitly state, invoking the Exceptions Clause has passed the two-thirds threshold in an advisory referendum, and the Supreme Court has struck down it or similar laws. Further, bills invoking the Exception Clause that have passed the two-thirds threshold in advisory referendums are not subject to Senate filibusters.

If the Supreme Court were to strike down a law that restores women's reproductive rights and secures women's right to purchase contraceptives and abortion pills, Congress could pass another bill that schedules an advisory referendum for voters to vote on using the Exceptions Clause to remove judicial review from all federal courts, including the Supreme Court, on cases involving women's reproductive rights.

Because some states will likely pass laws that violate the new law, Congress would have to create a special court to hear and rule on cases concerning women's reproductive rights. Congress has created courts several times.[38] Suppose this advisory referendum passes the two-thirds requirement. In that case, Congress should follow the same procedure described above to pass the law, remove judicial review from all federal courts, and establish a new human rights court to hear and rule on women's reproductive rights cases. Congress could staff the human rights court by reassigning federal judges, a process that Congress has also used several times.[39] If the President vetoes this bill, Democrats can promise to pass a law that guarantees women's reproductive rights and invokes the Exceptions Clause in 2029 when a Democrat occupies the White House.

Supreme Court Opens Floodgates on Campaign Spending

Corporations, despite being legal entities separate from their owners, have gained rights that were once exclusive to individuals. In 2010, the Supreme Court ruled 5-4 in *Citizens United* that laws limiting corporate election spending violate the Constitution. The court reasoned that corporations are entitled to the same First Amendment free speech protections as individuals and that spending money on elections is a form of speech. The ruling made over 100 years of laws restricting campaign donations from corporations, unions, and other organizations unconstitutional.[40] In 2014, the Supreme Court issued another five-to-four ruling in *McCutcheon v. FEC* that struck down the aggregate limits on the amount an individual may contribute during a two-year period to federal candidates, parties, and political action committees combined because those laws are unconstitutional under the First Amendment.[41]

After these rulings, corporations and the very rich, almost exclusively business owners and their heirs, could spend unlimited amounts on political campaigns provided they didn't "formally" coordinate with candidates or political parties. The vehicle for unlimited donating and spending is an independent expenditure-only political committee, also known as a super PAC.

To demonstrate the ridiculousness of the *Citizens United* ruling, late-night comedian Stephen Colbert formed a Super PAC and a shell company in Delaware to keep donations anonymous. Colbert then announced he was running for President of the United States of South Carolina. Because he could no longer legally manage his super PAC, he handed the Super PAC off to his comedian friend and business partner, Jon Stewart—all legal. Super PACs and election integrity had become a late-night joke.[42] [43] Like Colbert and Stewart, Super PACs are often run by candidates' friends, lawyers, and former campaign managers.[44]

After these rulings, money in politics exploded. In 2021, a ninety-year-old conservative billionaire gave $1.6 billion to the Marble Freedom Trust, a tax-exempt 501(c)(4) conservative advocacy organization run by Leonard Leo. Leo is an ultra-conservative Catholic who has played a leading role in staffing the Supreme Court with judges who oppose women's reproductive rights, voting rights, and climate change legislation. Wealthy donors prefer 501(c)(4)s because 501(c)(4)s don't have to disclose their donors. Marble Freedom Trust funnels its donations to Super PACs that support conservative causes and conservative politicians. Super PACs are required to disclose their donors so Super PAC money can be traced back to 501(c)(4)s, but not to the individuals or companies that contributed to the 501(c)(4)s.[45]

In the 2024 election cycle, America spent $15.9 billion on the federal election, or roughly forty times as much per capita as Germany and the UK spend on their federal elections.[46] Elon Musk alone spent $291 million to help reelect Donald Trump.

Five other business owners or their heirs spent over $100 million each to help elect Republicans.[47]

Billions more are spent on lobbying every year. In 2024, a record $4.4 billion was spent on federal lobbying, and 95 of the 100 highest-spending lobbyist organizations represent corporations.[48] Lobbyists bring their wealthy clients and politicians together by organizing fundraisers where corporate clients and wealthy individuals donate to candidates, including members of Congress, and to the Super-PACs that campaign for the candidates and against the candidates' opponents. Lobbyists then approach members of Congress with already-written legislation that benefits their clients and then shepherd their clients' bills through Congress.[49]

In *The System: Who Rigged It. How We Fix It,* author and former Labor Secretary, Robert Reich, states that unlimited political spending has increased the political power of corporations and the wealthy at the expense of everyone else.[50]

Following Trump's 2024 reelection, corporations and the rich scurried to gain his favor. Over $200 million was donated to the Trump/Vance Inaugural Committee, which broke the previous record of $107 million set by Trump/Pence for the 2017 inaugural. The Biden/Harris 2021 inaugural fund raised less than $62 million.[51] Amazon founder Jeff Bezos agreed to pay Melania Trump $40 million for her docuseries, an amount that was three times the next highest bid.[52] Trump rewarded Musk's donations by appointing him to lead the newly created Department of Government Efficiency (DOGE). DOGE indiscriminately fired federal workers and claimed large, often false, savings.

Several of the most politically active corporate interests (CEOs, corporate executives, owners, and heirs) do not want the same things most Americans want. Most Americans want good jobs, safe neighborhoods, good schools for their children, and affordable housing, healthcare, and education. On the other hand, these corporate interests flood campaigns and lobbyists with money to stop Congress from raising the minimum wage, lowering healthcare and housing costs, and adequately funding education and other public services.[53] Unfortunately, they have been remarkably successful at the expense of the quality of life for millions of Americans.

In 2025, the federal minimum wage of $7.25 per hour was just 57 percent what it was in 1971, adjusted for inflation. Further, low-paying temporary jobs exist in nearly every industry, and gig workers typically don't receive a guaranteed minimum wage, paid sick days, or health insurance.

The pharmaceutical industry's donors and lobbyists have been so effective that in 2022, U.S. prescription drug prices were, on average, 2.78 times as high as the average price in thirty-three other developed countries.[54] Healthcare costs are so high that there are still over half a million bankruptcies each year in America due to medical expenses, and 29 million Americans remain uninsured.[55]

With its corrupt influence over government officials, the financial industry has squeezed more money out of Main Street.

In the 1950s, the financial industry took $2.50 of every $100 spent. In 2019, the financial sector took $8.33 of every $100 spent.[56]

In 2025, 57 percent of Americans were living paycheck to paycheck because corporate interests have obtained what they wanted, while citizens have not.[57] That's 194 million people. People living paycheck to paycheck are at risk of not being able to pay bills if they miss a single payday. These are people who don't have enough savings to cover one large unexpected expense, such as a large hospital bill.

Further, trust in the government has declined. A 2014 poll indicated that 63 percent of Americans believed that most members of Congress would sell their vote for either cash or campaign contributions, and 59 percent thought their representative already had. In 1964, nearly two-thirds of Americans believed that the government was run for the benefit of all the people.[58]

The explosion of money in politics has also increased corruption. In 2023, the U.S. had dropped to 27th among 180 countries by Transparency International's Corruption Perception Index. America was perceived as more corrupt than Chile and the United Arab Emirates.[59]

This book predicts that if big money continues to dominate politics, wages will continue to stagnate, healthcare and housing costs will continue to skyrocket, and the quality of life for most Americans will continue to deteriorate.

Remove Big Money from Politics

Other democracies use various methods to limit the influence of big money on policy. The United Kingdom, Austria, Italy, and New Zealand limit campaign spending but allow unlimited contributions. Unlike America, British corporations and wealthy Brits are not allowed to spend unlimited amounts on elections. For the official ten-week Brexit campaign, each side received 600,000 pounds of public money, one free mailing to each household, and limited free TV time.[60] Each side was also allowed to spend just seven million pounds of their own funds. Australia, Denmark, Germany, Luxembourg, the Netherlands, Norway, Spain, Sweden, and Switzerland don't limit spending or contributions. But they forbid television advertising, provide a certain amount of TV time for free, provide public funding, and/or forbid candidates from campaigning until a relatively short time before election day.[61] Belgium, Canada, France, Iceland, Ireland, Israel, Japan, and South Korea limit both campaign donations and spending. France also forbids political contributions from corporations.[62]

America has the least election spending controls of any developed country and is, as a result, the most corrupt. In America, there are no limits on individual or corporate campaign donations to or spending by super PACs, no limits on television advertising, and no limits on campaign length.

Removing big money from politics will be difficult for two reasons. First, big-money donors and lobbyists can be counted on to spend a fortune to preserve their ability to manipulate elections and legislation. They will argue that campaign restrictions violate their First Amendment free-speech rights and claim that money is speech. Of course, money is not speech, and the Founding Fathers were so worried about the corrupting effects of money that Benjamin Franklin had to gain approval from Congress to accept a gift from King Louis XVI of France. The gift was a portrait of Louis surrounded by 408 diamonds in a golden case, sometimes called a snuff box.[63] Second, the Supreme Court stands ready to rule that laws restricting money are unconstitutional. Therefore, laws that restrict money in politics will need to invoke the Exceptions Clause.

This book recommends that a Democratic Congress pass a bill that schedules two advisory referendums, both on the same ballot, each requiring a two-thirds supermajority to pass. Advisory referendums will be needed even if Democrats have a sixty-vote majority in the Senate because passing an advisory referendum is required to invoke the Exceptions Clause (new rule #3).

The first bill should stipulate that non-humans, including corporations, unions, bots, artificial intelligence agents, and other non-humans, are prohibited from contributing to campaigns and other political organizations, including super PACs and party committees.

The second should limit the total individual contribution limit to candidates, party committees, PACs, political leadership PACs, super PACs, charities, lobbyists, and any other organization that contributes to political candidates or causes to $100,000 per year, a limit that increases with inflation. Lobbying would still be legal, but these restrictions would limit the amount of money lobbyists can donate to and raise for politicians' Super PACs, weakening lobbyists' power.

Both advisory referendums should state that the resulting laws will invoke the Exceptions Clause, which will remove judicial review from all federal courts, including the Supreme Court, and establish an anti-corruption court to hear and rule on cases involving election corruption.

Because of the new rule that bypasses the filibuster on bills that schedule advisory referendums, the bill should easily pass Congress. If President Trump vetoes the bill, Democrats can promise to remove big money from politics when a Democrat sits in the Oval Office.

If polls are correct and 88 percent of Americans support removing big money from politics, these advisory referendums should pass the two-thirds threshold. Congressional Democrats should again reach across the aisle and invite Republicans to vote for the bill because it carries out the will of the people. If there are fewer than sixty votes in favor in the Senate, Democrats can bypass the filibuster, justified by the new rule that the filibuster can be bypassed if the law in question passed a two-thirds threshold in an advisory referendum. If President Trump vetoes the bills, Democrats could promise to pass the legislation again when a Democrat sits in the Oval Office.

With big money removed from politics, Presidential candidates can accept federal funding. Everyone who files an individual tax return can check a box that donates $3 to the Presidential Election Campaign Fund (PECF). Eligible presidential candidates can use the money to help cover qualified expenses of their political campaigns in both the primary and general elections. To be eligible to receive public funds, the presidential nominee of a major party must agree to limit spending to $123.5 million in 2024 (the amount increases each election) and may not accept private contributions for the campaign.[64] From 1976 to 1996, all the major Presidential candidates participated in the PECF matching fund. After the *Citizens United* and *McCutcheon* rulings, unlimited fundraising became possible, making John McCain the last major party nominee to accept public financing through the PECF in 2008.[65]

With these election spending restrictions in place, it will be easier to pass legislation that improves the quality of life.

Advisory Referendums for a Better Democracy

Neither the Senate filibuster nor judicial review, particularly the Supreme Court's power to review and overturn laws made by Congress, originate in the Constitution. However, these powers have been used to stop and overturn legislation that improves the quality of life for Americans. Advisory referendums requiring a two-thirds supermajority to pass are recommended as a democratic justification for bypassing these two undemocratic processes.

Women Are People, Corporations Are Not

Nearly all democracies have used national votes to settle important policy questions. Twenty-six of the twenty-seven countries in the European Union have held national votes on policy. The only country that hasn't is Germany, which may be because of the stain of the referendums Hitler used to secure his dictatorship. However, Hitler's referendums were not free and fair elections. Referendums during the Nazi regime were ripe with voter intimidation and fraud.[66]

Opponents may argue that the Founding Fathers would oppose advisory referendums because they carefully considered national votes on policy and wisely rejected the idea, and that we should defer to them because they understood what was best for America for centuries to come. Thomas Jefferson, however, would disagree. On whether one generation has a right to bind another, he said, "The dead should not govern the living."[67] Further, the Founding Fathers demonstrated their flexibility when, after just seven years, they replaced the Articles of Confederation with the present Constitution. And the present Constitution includes something the Founding Fathers strongly opposed seven years earlier: a strong executive branch.[68] We'll never know what the Founding Fathers would do if they were alive today, but we know they took steps to prevent corruption.

Further, America already relies upon its citizens to make critical decisions. Trial by jury is a cornerstone of America's criminal justice system and is also required in many civil lawsuits. Jury trials are effective because jury tampering, such as bribing or intimidating jurors, is a crime often punished by prison. Imagine the corruption if plaintiffs, defendants, and prosecutors were, in the name of free speech, allowed to donate money to jurors and offer jurors high-paying jobs.

Finally, over 99 percent of Americans can legally vote directly on state or local government laws. In 2022, twenty-four states and 82 percent of America's 1,500 largest cities allowed initiatives, which allowed citizens and groups to have laws placed on the ballot by petition. Eleven states allow citizens and groups to modify their state constitutions by initiative.[69] (An initiative is a proposal originating from citizens that the electorate will vote on.)

Democracy v. Judicial Review

Other democracies do not grant their highest court as much power over the national legislature as the U.S. grants the Supreme Court. Great Britain, New Zealand, the Netherlands, Finland, Luxembourg, Sweden, and Switzerland do not grant their highest court the power to overturn laws made by their nations' legislature. These countries believe the legislature is the most appropriate arbiter of constitutional issues because it is the people's elected representative.

France has a Constitutional Council, not a court, that can be called on by the national assembly or the prime minister to determine the constitutionality of a law, but only after the legislature has passed it and only before it has been signed by the president.[70]

Canada and Denmark grant their highest court limited judicial review over laws made by their legislature. Canada's highest court has the power of judicial review, but the Canadian constitution contains a "Not Withstanding" clause that allows provincial and federal governments to continue to enforce a law even though it has been found unconstitutional. If the legislature feels that a court's ruling of unconstitutionality is mistaken or unreasonable, it can ignore that ruling for five years and renew that decision afterward. The Danish Supreme Court routinely defers to the constitutional interpretation of Parliament if it has some reasonable plausibility, even if that justification differs from what the court would have preferred. The Danish approach acknowledges that there can be more than one reasonable interpretation of a constitutional principle.[71] Norway's highest court can overturn laws that violate what the country's Constitution explicitly states.[72]

However, in the U.S., the Supreme Court has positioned itself as the final authority over laws made by Congress even if the text of the Constitution and the Amendments does not directly address the question before the Court. (Chapter 6 reveals the intent of the interpretive theory known as originalism that was used by the Supreme Court majority to decide *Dobbs* and *Citizens United*.)

The Supreme Court's power to review and overturn laws passed by Congress began in 1803 when the Supreme Court declared a law unconstitutional in *Marbury v. Madison*. Since then, judicial review has been a fundamental part of America's legal process. However, not all founders thought this was a good idea. Alexander Hamilton favored the idea. He wrote that courts must have the power to declare laws unconstitutional in Federalist Paper #78. Thomas Jefferson disagreed, stating, "To consider judges as the ultimate arbiters of all constitutional questions is a very dangerous doctrine indeed."[73]

Although the Constitution explicitly grants Congress the power to limit the Supreme Court's appellate jurisdiction, the Exceptions Clause has been used sparingly. Congress has invoked the Exceptions Clause to withhold judicial review from the Supreme Court on specific classes of cases, and the Supreme Court has found those laws constitutional.[74]

However, Congress has never used the Exceptions Clause to overturn a Supreme Court decision. Congress has tried several times, and a few efforts have passed the House of Representatives, but none have passed the Senate.[75]

Opponents of using the Exceptions Clause will likely argue that the Supreme Court's power to overturn laws passed by Congress should prevail because it is the precedent, and there is no telling what would happen without it. However, the economic success and high quality of life in the democratic countries listed above indicate that America would be just fine without it. Further, Congress's ability to invoke the Exceptions Clause to override extreme and unpopular Supreme Court rulings might motivate the Supreme Court to make fewer extreme and unpopular rulings.

Opponents will also argue that Democrats are simply trying to circumvent Supreme Court rulings they oppose. Proponents must be clear that using the Exceptions Clause is necessary because viable constitutional methods are needed to fix Supreme Court mistakes, and everyone makes mistakes. Without the Exceptions Clause, the methods available to overturn the Supreme Court's mistakes are future Supreme Court rulings, amendments, and civil wars. These are not preferred methods.

An advantage of democracies over dictatorships and monarchies is their ability to self-correct. Members of Congress and the President can be voted out. A common way voters tell a President they disapprove of their performance is by handing their party a drubbing in the midterm elections. However, Supreme Court justices and federal judges serve until retirement, death, or impeachment by the House and conviction by the Senate. To be a functioning democracy, America needs a check on the Supreme Court.

A Better Way

For years, undemocratic processes such as the Senate filibuster and the Supreme Court's judicial review have been used to obstruct the will of the people and harm the quality of life for millions of Americans.

Women Are People, Corporations Are Not

This chapter presents a moral, legal, and constitutional means of restoring women's reproductive rights and removing big money from politics. By restoring the basic elements of Roe throughout America, women in many states can regain their ability to fully participate in American life. By removing big money from politics, America can have a government of the people, by the people, and for the people.

Chapter 2

Better Health Through Affordable Healthcare

America has the highest per-capita healthcare cost and the lowest life expectancy in the developed world. In 2021, America was ranked last among eleven developed countries, way behind tenth-place Canada. Americans spend twice as much on healthcare per person as Canadians. (The eleven countries were the U.S., Canada, Switzerland, the Netherlands, the U.K., Norway, Germany, New Zealand, Australia, and France.)[76]

In 2023, America spent $4.9 trillion on healthcare, or $14,570 per person, which was 6.4 times the inflation-adjusted per-capital cost in 1971.[77] In 2024, the federal government spent $1.9 trillion on healthcare and services, or more than twice what was spent on defense.[78] A 2021 poll revealed that voters' number one priority was reducing healthcare costs.[79]

How We Got Here

On July 30, 1965, President Johnson signed into law the bill that led to Medicare and Medicaid. The original Medicare program included Part A (Hospital Insurance) and Part B (Medical Insurance: doctors). Today, these two parts are called "Original Medicare." Medicaid initially gave medical insurance to people who were getting cash assistance from the government. Today, a much larger group is covered: low-income families, pregnant women, people with disabilities, and people who need long-term care.[80]

In 1997, the Children's Health Insurance Program (CHIP) was created to provide health insurance and preventive care to uninsured American children.[81]

In 2003, the Medicare Prescription Drug Improvement and Modernization Act (MMA) made two significant changes. The Centers for Medicare & Medicaid Services (CMS) allowed private health insurance providers to create Medicare Advantage Plans or "Part C" Plans." Because of competition, Medicare Advantage was supposed to be cheaper than traditional Medicare. However, instead of saving taxpayers' money, Medicare Advantage has added tens of billions of dollars in costs.[82] One reason for the cost increases is that CMS allowed health insurance providers to add diagnoses to patients' records and receive larger payouts from Medicare.[83]

The MMA also expanded Medicare to include an optional prescription drug benefit, "Part D," that covers retail prescription drugs and went into effect in 2006.[84] In a gift to drug companies, the law included a provision known as the "noninterference" clause that prevented the Health and Human Services Department (HHS) from interfering with the negotiations between drug manufacturers, pharmacies, and prescription drug plans. The HHS also does not negotiate prices for drugs covered under Medicare Part B (administered by physicians). Instead, Medicare reimburses providers based on a formula set at 106 percent of the Average Sales Price (ASP), the average price to all non-federal purchasers in the U.S., including rebates.[85]

As a presidential candidate, Barack Obama promised to overhaul America's healthcare system. In 2009 and 2010, during the development of the Affordable Care Act, now known as Obamacare, the healthcare industry spent over a billion dollars to ensure there was no government option and that the government was not allowed to limit prices.[86] The bill's architect was Elizabeth Fowler, an advisor to Senator Max Bacus. She had previously worked as a top lobbyist for WellPoint, America's largest health insurance provider. After Obamacare's passage, Fowler accepted a senior-level position at Johnson & Johnson's government affairs and policy group.[87] This is an example of industry executives rotating between government and industry to help industries obtain legislation they desire.

In 2013, the Affordable Care Act went live. The law was supposed to eliminate or at least significantly reduce the burden of medical bills. Instead, healthcare costs increased rapidly.

From 2013 to 2023, healthcare spending per American increased 61 percent from $9,038 per person to $14,570.[88]

A Financial Burden for Employers and Employees

Healthcare has become so expensive that by 2022, employers paid more for healthcare as a percent of total employee compensation (7.9 percent) than they did for Social Security, Medicare, unemployment insurance, and worker's compensation benefits combined (7.2 percent). To reduce cost, employers have increased the share of premiums that employees pay and increased deductibles. Employees can fund health savings accounts with pre-tax dollars, if they enroll in HSA-qualifying high-deductible health plans. These cost reduction tactics harm low-income workers the most, and they do not address the real problem: healthcare cost too much.[89]

Small businesses have been especially burdened. From 2000 to 2023, the percentage of small businesses that offer healthcare to employees fell from 47 percent to 30 percent. According to the Affordable Care Act, businesses with fifty employees or less are not required to offer healthcare to their employees.[90]

A Small Step to Reduce Prescription Drug Costs

Roughly 42 percent of American adults are obese, the highest obesity rate in the developed world (obesity is defined as having a body mass index of 30 or higher).[91] A study estimated that nearly 500,000 Americans die prematurely every year due to obesity-related illnesses.[92]

In the last few years, people searching for weight loss have turned to the Type 2 diabetes drug Ozempic and the weight-loss drug Wegovy, both made by Novo Nordisk. Both use the same active ingredient: semaglutide. Wegovy contains more semaglutide than Ozempic. Semaglutide leads to weight loss by mimicking a naturally occurring hormone that tells your brain you are full. It also slows digestion by increasing the time it takes for food to leave the body. Insurers typically cover Ozempic for patients with Type 2 diabetes. However, insurers are less likely to cover Wegovy, or they may cover it for just a few months.[93]

Because there aren't any price controls in America, Novo Nordisk can charge what it wants. In 2025, the monthly cost of Ozempic without insurance was $936, or 11.28 times the monthly cost in France ($83), the lowest cost among the nine developed democracies that offer Ozempic and 5.54 times the monthly cost in Japan ($169), the highest cost among the nine developed democracies. The monthly cost for Wegovy was $1,349, 4.56 times the monthly cost in the Netherlands ($296) and 4.11 times the monthly cost in Germany ($328).[94] Germany and the Netherlands were the only other developed democracies offering Wegovy.

In 2022, U.S. prescription drug prices were, on average, 2.78 times higher than the average prices in thirty-three other developed countries, as noted.[95]

The first law that significantly addressed prescription drug costs is the Inflation Reduction Act of 2022. The law amended the non-interference clause by requiring the Secretary of HHS to negotiate prices with drug companies for a small number of single-source brand-name drugs or biologics without generic or biosimilar competitors covered under Medicare Part D (prescription drugs) and Part B. These are typically drugs with very high prices.[96]

Under the Drug Price Negotiation Program, the number of drugs selected for price negotiation is ten Part D drugs for 2026, another fifteen Part D drugs for 2027, another fifteen Part D and Part B drugs for 2028, and another twenty Part D and Part B drugs for 2029 and later years. The law also required that Part D plans limit the copayment to $35 per month for at least one type of insulin in at least one of each dosage form (vial, pen) and insulin type (rapid-acting, short-acting, intermediate-acting, and long-acting).[97]

The first ten drugs selected for negotiation are projected to save $6 billion in 2026, a 22 percent reduction in spending across these medications. In 2026, Medicare beneficiaries are expected to save $1.5 billion in out-of-pocket costs.[98] On January 17, 2025, CMS announced the selection of fifteen drugs covered under Medicare Part D for the second cycle of price negotiations that would go into effect in 2027. Ozempic and other weight loss drugs head the list. For the fiscal year from October 2023 to September 2024, weight loss drugs cost Medicare over $14 billion.[99]

Several drug companies and pharmaceutical trade organizations brought lawsuits in federal courts against the provision in the Inflation Reduction Act that requires the Secretary of HHS to negotiate prices with drug companies, claiming it is unconstitutional under the First, Fifth, and Eighth Amendments. These lawsuits appear frivolous because the government that pays them has every right to negotiate prices. As of this writing, none of the plaintiffs have won, and the law stands.[100]

Compared to other developed democracies, this is small progress. But in America, it is a significant victory over the powerful pharmaceutical lobby, made possible by the fact that 83 percent of voters want the government to lower the cost of prescription drugs.

Accelerate and Expand Prescription Drug Price Reductions

Accelerating the number of drugs negotiated from fifteen to thirty beginning in 2027 could add $50 million in savings annually to Medicare. Extending negotiated drug prices to Medicaid and private insurance plans could bring annual savings to $100 million.[101] This book recommends that Democrats commit to passing this bill.

The pharmaceutical industry will fight this bill with every means at its disposal, even if big money is removed from politics. There will be a media assault, calling it government overreach, Soviet-style central planning, and the end of capitalism.

However, the government has done much to create America's large and highly profitable pharmaceutical industry. First, the National Institute of Health (NIH) provides billions of dollars yearly to drug companies. From 2010 to 2019, the NIH spent $187 billion on basic or applied research related to 354 of the 356 drugs approved by the Food and Drug Administration (FDA). On average, the NIH spent roughly as much on each approved first-in-class drug ($1.4 billion) as the drug company that sold it ($1.5 billion).[102] Second, government patent laws grant drug companies twenty-year monopolies. This book merely recommends that the government rein in drug companies that have taken advantage of their monopoly status to charge exorbitant prices.

A bill that accelerates and expands prescription drug price reductions would not be subject to the Senate filibuster if it were considered budget reconciliation, which the Inflation Reduction Act was. If the filibuster does not apply and big money is removed from politics, a Democratic Congress could pass the bill with a simple majority in the Senate. However, if the pharmaceutical industry remains the powerful force it is today or justification is needed for a filibuster exception, this book recommends that Democrats pass a bill that schedules an advisory referendum to demonstrate overwhelming voter support for this law. If President Trump vetoes the bill,

Democrats can promise to pass the law when a Democrat sits in the Oval Office.

If the polls are correct, this advisory referendum should pass the two-thirds threshold. Congressional Democrats should again reach across the aisle and invite Republicans to vote for the bill because it has overwhelming support from voters. If the bill does not qualify as budget reconciliation and there are fewer than sixty votes in favor in the Senate, Democrats can bypass the filibuster due to the new rule that allows the filibuster to be bypassed if the law in question has passed the two-thirds threshold in an advisory referendum. If President Trump vetoes the bills, he exposes himself for opposing legislation that voters overwhelmingly support, and the Democrats could promise to pass the legislation again when a Democrat sits in the Oval Office.

Once passed, this law will generate an avalanche of lawsuits, arguing that the government has no right to interfere with the current price negotiations between drug makers and private insurance companies, pharmacies, and others. The Supreme Court has upheld laws that control prices, but the current Supreme Court has not hesitated to rule against precedent.

If the Supreme Court were to strike down the law, Democrats in Congress might be able to draft and pass a new law that accommodates the Court's objections. If not, Democrats should schedule another advisory referendum that asks voters if they support invoking the Exceptions Clause to let the law stand and to create a healthcare pricing court with reassigned federal judges to adjudicate matters related to prescription drug prices.

Hospitals Overcharge

In 2022, spending on hospital services accounted for 42 percent of total healthcare spending among the 160 million Americans with private insurance.[103] The price paid to hospitals for privately insured individuals was, on average, 2.54 times what Medicare would have paid. Hospital costs are the primary reason healthcare costs cause financial distress and bankruptcy.

Hospital costs vary widely among states. Arkansas, Iowa, Massachusetts, Michigan, and Mississippi had prices under twice what Medicare would have paid. California, Florida, Georgia, New York, South Carolina, West Virginia, and Wisconsin had prices above three times what Medicare would have paid. Maryland was the only state where privately insured and Medicare recipients paid the same price.[104]

The financial industry has driven much of the cost increases in hospitals. Wall Street firms, such as private equity firms, have bought hospitals and raised prices. In 2022, one of every three medical personnel working in America's emergency rooms worked for two private equity companies: Blackstone and Kohlberg Kravis Roberts & Co. With private equity in charge, emergency room doctors ordered more expensive tests and surprised patients with out-of-network costs.[105] According to the Wall Street Journal, "price increases are a key tool for private equity firms to boost profits at companies they acquire."[106]

Reduce Hospital Costs

Seventy-eight percent of voters support a law that limits hospitals from charging more than twice what Medicare allows.[107] This book recommends that Democrats draft a bill that limits what hospitals can charge to twice what Medicare would pay after two years and the same as what Medicare would pay after five years. Hospitals that fail to reach these goals would face fines. Limiting what hospitals can charge to what Medicare would pay will reduce healthcare costs by roughly $800 billion annually by 2032.

Like laws limiting drug prices, the hospital services industry and its Wall Street owners will fight this bill with every means at their disposal, even if big money is removed from politics.

This bill would also be exempt from the Senate filibuster if it is considered budget reconciliation. If big money is not removed or the bill is not exempt from the filibuster, Democrats could add what hospitals can charge on the same advisory referendum ballot as accelerating and expanding prescription drug negotiation. If the polls are correct, this advisory referendum should pass the two-thirds threshold. A Democratic Congress could then add this bill to the prescription drug bill, bypass the filibuster, and send the bill to the President. If he vetoes it, Democrats could promise to pass the legislation again when a Democrat sits in the Oval Office.

Once passed, this law will also generate an avalanche of lawsuits, arguing that the government has no right to interfere with free-market pricing. If the Supreme Court were to strike down the law, Democrats in Congress might be able to draft and pass a new law that accommodates the Court's objections. If not, Democrats should schedule another advisory referendum that asks voters if they support invoking the Exceptions Clause to let the law stand, using the healthcare pricing court mentioned above to adjudicate matters related to prescription drug prices.

Rampant Medicare and Medicaid Fraud

Medicare and Medicaid fraud are estimated to exceed $100 billion per year. There are two primary types of Medicare and Medicaid fraud. First is making claims for services not rendered. All it takes is a street address, patient information, doctors' signatures, and the government-issued Medicare and Medicaid handbooks that explain how to charge the government for services rendered or, in this case, not rendered. Fraudsters can purchase patient and doctor information, and corrupt doctors can be part of the scheme. Fraudsters merely invoice Medicare and Medicaid for tests, medical equipment, and treatments that never took place. Clinics with empty storefronts and no employees sprout like weeds in strip malls across America. Ground zero is South Florida.[108]

The second is insurance provider overbilling. As noted, Medicare pays private insurance companies more for patients with conditions that are expensive to treat. For instance, Medicare pays private insurers an annual base rate of $3,735 for a healthy person. But if someone is diagnosed with morbid obesity, Medicare adds $2,370 for a total of $6,105.[109]

According to the New York Times, Kaiser Permanente called its doctors during lunch and after work and urged them to add illnesses to the medical records of patients they hadn't seen in weeks. Doctors who found enough new diagnoses could earn bottles of champagne or a bonus in their paycheck. Anthem paid more to doctors who said their patients were sicker. And executives at UnitedHealth Group told their workers to search through old medical records for more illnesses, and when they couldn't find enough, they sent them back to try again. Many patients and their doctors never find out that they have been misdiagnosed by their insurers.

Six of the ten largest health insurance companies have been accused of fraud by either whistleblowers or the U.S. government. According to federal audits, eight of the ten biggest Medicare Advantage insurers, representing more than two-thirds of the market, have submitted inflated bills to Medicare. Four of the five most prominent players, UnitedHealth, Humana, Elevance, and Kaiser, have faced federal lawsuits alleging that efforts to over-diagnose their customers crossed the line into fraud. Overbilling estimates are as high as $25 billion per year. For comparison, NASA's budget is $21.5 billion.[110]

Reduce Medicare and Medicaid Fraud

Some types of Medicare fraud should be easy to stop. It should be easy to stop Medicare Advantage insurance providers from adding false maladies to patients' records. This book predicts that Republicans would join Democrats to pass a law prohibiting insurance providers from adding maladies to patients' records. If Medicare Advantage insurance providers believe patients have additional maladies, they should contact the patients. This could save up to $25 billion per year. This book predicts the Supreme Court will let this law stand.

Stopping false Medicare claims is much harder. There are 450 federal agents assigned to Medicare and Medicaid fraud, but they can't begin to keep up.[111] Having more agents would help, and the additional agents might recover more money than they would cost. However, this book does not recommend any policies that require tax increases, as noted.

Better Health Through Affordable Healthcare

In 2023, America spent $14,570 per person, which was 6.4 times the inflation-adjusted per-capital cost in 1971. Enacting these three laws would reduce the cost of healthcare by nearly one trillion dollars per year by 2032. Most importantly, the burden of large medical bills would be greatly reduced, resulting in fewer healthcare bankruptcies. These laws would also significantly reduce employer healthcare costs and shore up Medicare, Medicaid, and other government-funded healthcare.

Chapter 3

Affordable Housing

In 2007, two Bear Stearns hedge funds filled with mortgage-backed securities went bankrupt, a German bank filled with mortgage-backed securities was bailed out, credit ratings agencies downgraded nearly $200 billion in mortgage-backed securities and derivatives, and 14 percent of subprime mortgages were seriously delinquent, up from 6 percent at the beginning of 2006.[112] [113] [114] The stage was set for the worst financial crisis since the Great Depression. This crisis, however, could have been easily avoided.

> Like the story of the scorpion and the frog, all the banks had to do to survive was allow struggling homeowners to refinance, lower their interest rates and monthly payments, and keep their homes. Instead, banks couldn't resist foreclosing and taking homes from millions of Americans.

Affordable Housing

In spring 2007, Bear Stearns and other Wall Street banks whose mortgage-backed securities had lost value announced plans to buy and forgive delinquent loans in their mortgage-backed securities. This would keep homeowners in their homes and save Bear Stearns and other Wall Street banks billions in losses. However, this plan was strongly opposed by hedge fund managers who were betting against mortgage-backed securities. Lawsuits were threatened, and the plan was dropped. A year later, Bear Stearns was gone.[115]

Most homeowners had planned to refinance before subprime adjustable interest rates jumped and monthly mortgage payments skyrocketed. But they couldn't because the companies that sold subprime loans had either failed or were failing.[116] Had banks allowed homeowners to refinance, many homeowners could have kept their homes, the rapid decrease in the value of real estate and mortgage-backed securities could have been slowed, and the financial crisis, Great Recession, and government bailouts could have been mostly avoided.

Federal Deposit Insurance Company (FDIC) Chairman Sheila Bair tried multiple times to allow struggling homeowners to refinance and keep their homes. In 2007, Bair proposed converting adjustable-rate loans to thirty-year mortgages at low teaser interest rates. After months of negotiation and compromise with other regulators, the Federal Reserve, and the Treasury Department, the government announced the voluntary Hope Now Alliance that qualified 1.8 million homeowners for a streamlined process that would extend the

Affordable Housing

teaser interest rate period by five years. However, Wall Street used its veto authority to opt out or slow down the program so that only a few hundred thousand mortgages were modified.[117]

In 2008, Sheila Bair proposed that the government provide low-interest loans to borrowers with unaffordable mortgages, where mortgage payments exceeded 40 percent of the borrower's gross income. Wall Street opposed the program, and the Treasury Department vetoed the idea, claiming that the government should not bail out homeowners.[118]

President Obama promised to provide relief to the millions of Americans who were at risk of losing their homes. With the President's support, Sheila Bair proposed a loan modification program called the Home Affordable Mortgage Program (HAMP). President Obama predicted that HAMP would help three to four million struggling homeowners. Bair proposed a simple loan modification process because struggling homeowners had already qualified for their mortgages. However, Treasury Secretary Timothy Geithner and National Economic Council Leader Larry Summers insisted on a qualification process that was so complex that only half a million homeowners had modified their loans two years later.

As a candidate, Obama promised to change bankruptcy laws to help families stay in their homes. Bankruptcy judges are barred from lowering mortgage payments on primary residences, even though they can lower payments on nearly every other type of debt, including mortgages on vacation homes. Candidate Obama called the current law "the kind of out-of-touch Washington loophole that makes no sense." However, the entire financial industry, from Wall Street to community banks, opposed the action. In 2009, a bill allowing distressed homeowners to use bankruptcy to reduce their debt passed the House of Representatives. In the Senate, twelve Democrats joined the Republicans to vote down the bill.[119]

Banks wanted the houses, even if it killed them, and they got them. By 2011, 4.7 million American households had lost their homes. For real estate investment firms, the extraordinary supply of cheap homes in good neighborhoods was a once-in-a-lifetime opportunity. Real Estate Investment Trusts (REITs) were funded with money from around the world, including Qatar, the Korean Exchange Bank, the Cayman Islands, the British Virgin Islands, Columbia University, and the California Public Employees' Retirement System. Private equity firms took the lead. Blackstone, the largest private equity company in the world, amassed 82,500 homes.[120]

REITs focused their buying spree on cities with growing populations, including Phoenix, Atlanta, Las Vegas, Miami, Charlotte, Los Angeles, and Denver. These cities had an abundance of cheap houses and high rental demand. As the economy recovered, housing prices skyrocketed partly because so many homes had been taken off the market. Because private equity firms aim to maximize profit, rent prices were increased, fees were added, maintenance was delayed, and renters who fell behind were quickly evicted.[121]

Affordable Housing

In 2022, large institutional investors (companies that own over 100 single-family homes) owned 574,000 single-family homes, including 29 percent of single-family-rental homes in Atlanta, 24 percent in Jacksonville, Florida, and 20 percent in Charlotte, North Carolina.[122]

Private equity firms have also purchased thousands of apartment complexes. Blackstone alone owns over 200,000 units. Again, renters suffered through rent increases, fees, delayed maintenance, and evictions.[123]

Today, housing costs eat up much of the budget for millions of Americans. Nearly 30 percent of American homeowners are "house poor," meaning they spend 30 or more percent of their income on housing. Forty percent of renters spend over 30 percent of their income on housing.[124]

Sell the Houses Back to Homeowners

In 2023, House and Senate Democrats drafted bills requiring corporate owners to sell all of their single-family homes to would-be homeowners over ten years. The bills would add thousands of single-family homes to the supply in cities that desperately need them. Naturally, Wall Street opposed the idea. The CEO of the National Rental Home Council, a trade association, said, "Wall Street is not the problem; a lack of new housing is." In other words, "We took your houses through legitimate means: lobbying and campaign donations. If you want houses, build new ones." The bills didn't make it very far, which should not be a surprise because the people who own private equity firms spend fortunes on campaign donations and lobbying.[125] [126]

If big money is removed from politics and Democrats have sixty votes in the Senate, Democrats could pass a bill that requires corporate owners to sell their homes. If not, this book recommends that Democrats pass a bill that schedules another advisory referendum. The advisory referendum should state that corporate owners of more than fifty single-family homes must sell them within three years. The time frame is short because cities desperately need more single-family homes on the market.

This book predicts that this advisory referendum would pass the two-thirds threshold. Senate Democrats could then make a filibuster exception, and Congress could pass the bill. Corporate owners would be fined $50,000 for each home over fifty they own after three years.

If President Trump vetoes the bill that schedules the advisory referendum or the bill that requires corporate owners to sell their homes, Democrats could promise to pass the legislation again when a Democrat sits in the Oval Office.

The courts should let this law stand.

Build Affordable Houses and Apartments

The CEO of the National Rental Home Council was correct about one thing. America needs to build more houses. America

Affordable Housing

has roughly 425 dwellings (houses, condominiums, and apartments, etc.) per thousand people. Italy, France, Portugal, and Finland have between 580 and 600 dwellings per thousand people. The average in the European Union is about 520.[127]

The shortage of houses, particularly affordable houses, combined with stagnant wages have caused housing prices to increase more than four times faster than income. From 1971 to 2023, the median price of a home increased from $25,200 to $428,700, a seventeen-fold increase while the median salary only increased from $10,622 to $44,225, a four-fold increase.[128]

As Ezra Klein and Derek Thompson write in *Abundance*, housing prices have soared because many American communities have used regulations, zoning, and burdensome permitting processes to restrict the supply of homes, require expensive features, and exclude high-density apartments and rooming houses for down-on-their-luck citizens to increase the value of their homes and their net worths.

The housing problem is worse in states run by Democrats. In 2024, the median house price in San Francisco was $1.3 million, Los Angeles was $1 million, Seattle was $900,000, and Boston was $830,000. California has made it extremely difficult to obtain permits to build houses, apartments, high-speed rail, and just about anything else. In the Los Angeles and San Francisco metro areas, just 2.5 new housing permits were issued in 2022 per 1,000 residents. In Austin, Texas, there were eighteen. As a result, California has high housing prices, high cost of living, and high levels of homelessness.[129]

Because of the high cost of living, the largest Democratic states are losing residents. In 2023, California's population decreased by 342,000, New York's by 284,000, and Illinois' by 115,000.[130] Because fewer people are paying taxes, these states are under pressure to raise taxes to pay for services, which motivates more people to leave. Worse for Democrats is the criticism that they can't get things done.

Finally, there appears to be recognition that there is too much bureaucracy. In June 2025, California's legislature passed two laws that rolled back its 1970 environmental law that has been blamed for much of California's inability to build low-cost housing and nearly anything else. The California Environmental Quality Act of 1970 was initially written to apply principally to government projects. However, a 1972 state court decision expanded it to apply to many private projects as well. For years, the law has been used by environmentalists, neighbors, and disgruntled parties to delay and stop projects they found objectionable.[131]

Affordable Housing

From 1971 to 2023, housing prices rose more than four times faster than income. Requiring corporate owners to sell hundreds of thousands of homes to homeowners is a first step in lowering the cost of housing. States should reform their laws and regulations to allow faster permitting and construction of affordable houses and apartments.

Chapter 4

Raise Minimum Wage

Since 1938, the federal minimum wage has been raised twenty-three times, counting the creation of a minimum wage as the first raise. It was raised twenty-one times by laws passed by Democratic congresses and twice by Republican congresses. The minimum wage has never been raised when the Republicans controlled both Congress and the Presidency. The federal minimum wage was last raised to $7.25 per hour in 2009 when Democrats controlled both Congress and the Presidency.[132]

In 2021, the Democrats controlled both houses of Congress and the White House for the first time since 2011. The House passed the American Rescue Plan Act of 2021 (COVID-19 relief) with a plan to gradually raise the federal minimum wage to $15 per hour by 2025. The bill would have increased wages for 32 million Americans. However, the Senate parliamentarian ruled that raising the minimum wage, unlike the COVID-19 relief bill, required sixty votes to overcome the filibuster. Senate Democrats tried to overrule the filibuster, but the vote failed, and the federal minimum wage remained at $7.25 per hour. At the time, twenty-one states used the federal minimum as their minimum wage. In all those states, $7.25 per hour fell short of a living wage without government programs.[133] From 2009 to 2025, cumulative inflation was 49 percent, which reduced the purchasing power of the dollar by roughly one-third.

> Example: In 2009, $7.25 (one hour working at the minimum wage) could buy seven hot dogs priced at $1.00 each, with twenty-five cents left over. In 2025, hot dogs cost 49 percent more, or $1.49 each, and $7.25 can only buy four hot dogs with $1.29 left over.

Walmart Increased Poverty

In 2014, a study revealed that Walmart employees received $6.2 billion from government poverty programs. The combination of minimum-wage pay and Walmart's thirty-four-hour full-time workweek qualified thousands of Walmart employees for taxpayer-funded Medicaid, food stamps, Section 8 housing, and earned income tax credit, among other government programs. The $6.2 billion was 27 percent of Walmart's 2014 U.S. operating income.[134] [135]

Walmart's effect on communities has been studied extensively, and the data showed that poverty increased after Walmart arrived. This should not be a surprise because

Raise Minimum Wage

Walmart pays many of its employees' incomes below the poverty line. Further, Walmart's suppliers were expected to reduce prices yearly, resulting in outsourcing to countries with lower-cost labor, costing Americans more jobs. Four of Walmart's ten largest suppliers in 1994 eventually entered bankruptcy. A fifth was bought by a private equity company to avoid bankruptcy. By the early 2000s, twenty-nine of Walmart's competitors (grocery chains), nearly all of which paid higher wages than Walmart, had been forced into bankruptcy.[136] At the same time, the Walton family, the heirs of founder Sam Walton, have become the wealthiest family in the world.[137]

In 2021, 25 million Americans received an average of $2,411 from the Earned Income Tax Credit, costing taxpayers $60.3 billion. The strongest supporters of these programs are Walmart, the U.S Chamber of Commerce, fast food, and other companies that don't pay their workers a living wage. However, the government has made applying for these programs so difficult that billions of dollars are left unclaimed every year. Walmart and a few other companies proactively help their workers apply for these government programs. These government low-income subsidies provide Walmart and other companies that don't pay a living wage with a competitive advantage against companies that do pay a living wage.

Opposition to Minimum Wage

In 1946, eight years after the minimum wage became law, a future Nobel Prize-winning economist named George Stigler wrote a paper claiming that raising the minimum wage was bad because higher wages would result in fewer workers. Stigler didn't have evidence to support this conclusion, but his theory became an economic teaching in many textbooks and continues to be taught today.[138]

In 1992, New Jersey raised its minimum wage while its neighbor, Pennsylvania, did not. If Stigler was correct, New Jersey minimum-wage industries should have lost workers while Pennsylvania minimum-wage industries should not. Two Princeton economists studied 410 fast food restaurants in each state. They found that the higher minimum wage in New Jersey made no difference in the employment numbers of fast-food workers.[139]

In 2023, California raised the wages for workers at fast-food chains with sixty or more locations to $20 per hour and created new health and safety standards. Opponents again predicted massive layoffs and business closures. Instead, California added 11,000 new jobs in the fast-food industry, and many fast-food workers could pay rent and buy food.[140]

Raise the Minimum Wage

Once in control of Congress, Democrats should pass the Raise the Wage Act, a bill drafted by Congressional Democrats in 2025 that gradually raises the federal minimum wage to $17 per hour by 2030 and gradually raise the minimum wage for tipped

Raise Minimum Wage

workers, workers with disabilities, and youth workers.[141] (The current federal minimum wage for tipped workers is $2.13.)

If big money is removed from politics and Democrats have sixty votes in the Senate, Congress should quickly prepare this bill and send it to the President. If not, this book recommends that Democrats pass a bill scheduling an advisory referendum.

If the polls are correct, the bill would pass the two-thirds threshold, Senate Democrats could then bypass the filibuster, and a Democratic Congress could pass the bill. If the President vetoes the bill scheduling an advisory referendum or the bill raising the minimum wage, Democrats could promise to pass the legislation again when a Democrat sits in the Oval Office, and millions of underpaid Americans could receive a raise.

This book predicts that the Supreme Court would let a minimum wage law stand.

Ensuring Ride-Sharing Drivers Earn a Living Wage

Unions and progressives have tried multiple times to classify gig workers as employees. Thus far, voters, including voters in California, prefer that gig workers remain contractors.

In September 2019, California Governor Gavin Newsom signed Assembly Bill 5, a law that extended wage and benefit protections to about a million workers, most of whom were drivers contracted by ride-hailing companies. Newsom said the new law "will help reduce worker misclassification—workers being wrongly classified as 'independent contractors' rather than employees, which erodes basic worker protections like the minimum wage, paid sick days, and health insurance benefits." The bill covers workers in various industries, including health care, trucking, and media. Some industries, such as real estate, commercial fishing, and cosmetology services, carved out exemptions from the law. However, the app-based tech companies, primarily Uber, Lyft, and DoorDash, were not granted exemptions.[142]

After the bill was signed into law, Uber announced it would not comply. Instead, its drivers would remain contractors. Uber, along with Lyft and DoorDash, then promised to spend $90 million on a 2020 ballot measure to exempt their drivers from California's Assembly Bill 5. A "yes" vote on Proposition 22 would keep drivers classified as contractors, and a "no" vote would reclassify drivers as employees.[143]

Although a "Yes" vote would keep ride-sharing and delivery drivers classified as contractors, drivers would be guaranteed 120 percent of the state-mandated minimum wage for "engaged time," defined as the time between accepting a ride or delivery request and completing the trip.[144] Drivers would also receive $0.30 per mile for vehicle expenses, which increases annually with inflation. Proposition 22 would also establish a quarterly health care subsidy for drivers depending on their hours.[145] Because drivers remained contractors, Uber, Lyft, and other ride-sharing companies would continue to not pay social security, Medicare, and unemployment taxes.

Raise Minimum Wage

It was a hotly contested campaign in which sharing companies outspent the opposition $200 million to $20 million. On November 3, 2020, Prop. 22 won with 58 percent of the vote, allowing Uber, Lyft, and other sharing companies to continue classifying workers as independent contractors.[146] In 2021, a nationwide poll showed that 62 percent of voters see gig workers as contractors, and just 35 percent see them as employees.[147]

Proponents of making drivers employees vowed to fight on. However, 84 percent of drivers said they would rather be contractors of ride-sharing and delivery firms than employees, and 76 percent said they benefited personally from Prop. 22.[148] In 2023, California's ride-sharing and delivery drivers received an automatic raise when California raised its minimum wage to $20 per hour.

Consider Prop. 22 Nationwide as a Minimum Benefit for Drivers

California's Prop. 22 isn't perfect. It does not provide drivers with unemployment insurance, sick days, or overtime pay. However, combined with an increase in the minimum wage, it would help Uber, Lyft, and DoorDash drivers in many states. Democrats could survey voters throughout America to determine how much support exists for a bill modeled after Prop. 22.

If there is strong support and Democrats have sixty votes in the Senate, they could pass such a bill and send it to the President. If Democrats don't have sixty votes in the Senate, they could pass a bill that schedules an advisory referendum. If the advisory referendum passes the two-thirds threshold, Democrats can pass a bill and send it to the President. If President Trump vetoes the bill that schedules the advisory referendum or the bill modeled after California's Prop 22, Democrats could promise to pass the legislation again when a Democrat sits in the Oval Office, and thousands of ride-sharing and delivery drivers could receive a raise. This book predicts that the Supreme Court would not overturn this law.

Higher Minimum Wage Improves Quality of Life

In 2025, federal minimum wage of $7.25 per hour was just 57 percent of what it was in 1971 adjusted for inflation. Raising the minimum wage to $17 per hour by 2030 combined with a national law modeled after California's Prop. 22 would raise income for millions of Americans. According to Matthew Desmond, author of, *Poverty in America*, raising the minimum wage eases the "grind of poverty." It reduces stress-related health problems, teen births, child neglect, smoking, and alcohol consumption.[149]

Chapter 5

Advance Democracy

America's democracy is in decline. According to the Carnegie Endowment for International Peace, "Every major international measure of democracy demonstrates serious U.S. decline." In 2017, the Economist Intelligence Unit downgraded the United States to a "flawed democracy." Europe's International Institute for Democracy and Electoral Assistance classified the United States as a "backsliding democracy." The Freedom House shows the United States on one of the fastest downward trajectories of any country, now ranking U.S. democratic quality alongside Romania and Croatia.[150]

This chapter describes three recent Supreme Court rulings that have compromised democracy against the will of the people and how Democrats could fix them. It also describes how to eliminate the electoral college without an amendment.

Restore the Voting Rights Act

The Voting Rights Act of 1965 (VRA) prohibited racial discrimination in voting. The law outlawed discriminatory practices like literacy tests and poll taxes. It stipulated that nine states and several counties with the worst history of African American voter disenfranchisement must obtain federal judge approval before changing their voter laws. The VRA has been renewed multiple times, the last time in 2006 by a vote of 330 to 33 in the House and 98 to 0 in the Senate.[151]

In 2013, the year after President Obama was reelected, the Supreme Court struck down, by a 5 to 4 vote, the provision in the VRA that stipulated that the nine states and several counties needed a federal judge's approval before changing their voter laws.[152] In its *Shelby v. Holder* ruling, Chief Justice John Roberts concluded that the VRA provision was no longer needed because "African-American voter turnout exceeded white voter turnout in five of the six states originally covered by the provision" and "Congress must ensure that the legislation it passes to remedy that problem speaks to current conditions."[153] Had the provision not been in place, Obama would have had a more difficult path to the Presidency. Supreme Court logic held that the provision in the VRA that outlawed voting discrimination was unconstitutional because it prevented voting discrimination. By 2021, twenty-six states had passed restrictive voting laws.[154]

In 2019, House Democrats passed the Voting Rights Advancement Act. However, Republicans controlled the

Senate, and Mitch McConnell refused to allow floor debate or a vote. After winning both houses of Congress and the Presidency in 2020, Democrats tried again. In 2021, the House Democrats passed a similar bill called the John Lewis Voting Rights Act, named after the recently passed Congressman and civil rights leader. The bill included provisions to keep the list of states and counties that need federal judge approval current, which Democrats hoped would resolve the Supreme Court's objection. The bill was blocked in the Senate by the filibuster. Two months later, House Democrats folded the John Lewis Voting Rights Act into the broader Freedom to Vote Act that established same-day voter registration and expanded early voting. Senate Democrats again failed to overrule a Republican filibuster.[155]

A 2022 survey revealed that 63 percent of Americans supported the John Lewis Voting Rights Act.[156] This book recommends that Congressional Democrats draft the John Lewis Voting Rights Act again with two provisions attached. First is a voter-friendly ID requirement. Democrats have opposed voter ID bills for years, arguing that voter fraud is extremely rare. Nevertheless, 80 percent of voters support requiring voters to show government-issued photo IDs.[157] A provision could make it free and easy for citizens to obtain a photo ID from the federal government. The second provision requires paper ballot backups for electronic voting machines, and over 80 percent of voters support that, too.[158] By adding these provisions, Democrats could establish themselves as champions of free and fair elections and hopefully motivate enough Republicans to vote for the bill that it achieves the sixty votes required to stop a filibuster in the Senate. If not, Democrats could pass a bill that schedules an advisory referendum.

This book predicts that the John Lewis Voting Rights Act, with the two provisions, would pass the two-thirds threshold and justify bypassing the filibuster. If the President vetoes the bill scheduling the advisory referendum or the bill restoring the Voting Rights Act, Democrats could promise to pass the legislation again when a Democrat sits in the Oval Office.

Once signed into law, this book predicts that the Supreme Court will let it stand because the John Lewis bill accommodates the Court's objection.

Ban Gerrymandering

Gerrymandering is one of the most effective methods of rigging elections. Gerrymandering occurs when one political party draws electoral districts in its own favor, skewing the makeup of Congress and state legislatures, and creating a legislative body that does not represent voters' preferences. A common tactic is "packing" voters likely to favor the opposing party into fewer districts.[159]

Hungary's Prime Minister, Viktor Orban, has used gerrymandering to remain in power. In Hungary's last two elections, Orban's political party, Fidesz, received less than half of the votes but won roughly two-thirds of the parliamentary seats. Orban has essentially become a dictator by taking over the courts, the media, and parliament.[160]

Both Democrats and Republicans gerrymander, but Republicans are better at it. After the 2010 census, several states with Republican-controlled governments gerrymandered their districts. In the 2012 election, Democratic House of Representatives candidates won 48.8 percent of the national vote and Republicans won 47.6 percent, but Republicans achieved a forty-nine-seat House majority of 242 to 193.[161]

The Supreme Court has made gerrymandering easier. In 2019, the Supreme Court ruled in *Rucho v. Common Cause* and *Lamone v. Benisek* that claims of unconstitutional partisan gerrymandering are not subject to federal court review. The Court acknowledged two areas relating to redistricting where the Supreme Court has a role in policing the states: racial gerrymandering and grossly unequal population among districts. The Court suggested that Congress could play a role in regulating partisan gerrymandering.[162] In other words, Congress could pass a law.

Following the 2020 census, South Carolina Republicans moved 30,000 African American voters from a district the Republicans didn't want to lose to a district 100 miles away that Republicans were already losing. The South Carolina Conference of the NAACP challenged the map in federal district court. The three-judge district court ruled unanimously that the South Carolina legislature engaged in unconstitutional racial gerrymandering, a violation of the 14th Amendment.[163]

Thomas Alexander, President of the South Carolina Senate, appealed to the Supreme Court. In May 2024, in *Alexander v. South Carolina NAACP,* the Supreme Court ruled six to three along partisan lines to overturn the district court's ruling. The Court ruled that the redrawn map was a partisan gerrymander, not a racial gerrymander, and the *Rucho* ruling prevents federal courts from hearing cases on partisan gerrymandering.[164]

A poll showed that 70 percent of voters want the Supreme Court to stop partisan gerrymandering. Democrats have drafted multiple bills to ban gerrymandering. In 2021, House Democrats passed the For the People Act. The bill would ban partisan gerrymandering, restore the Voting Rights Act, expose dark money by requiring any organization involved in political activity to disclose its large donors, slow the revolving door, prevent Members of Congress from serving on corporate boards, and require presidential candidates to disclose their tax returns.[165] In a Senate procedural vote, all fifty Democrats voted for the bill and all fifty Republicans voted against. The Democrats again lacked the votes to overcome the filibuster, and two Democratic Senators, Joe Machin and Kyrsten Sinema, opposed bypassing the filibuster.[166]

This book recommends that Democrats pass a bill that bans partisan gerrymandering only. Everyone knows gerrymandering is wrong. There may be enough Republicans voting for the bill that it achieves the sixty votes required to stop the Senate filibuster. If not, Congressional Democrats could pass a bill that schedules an advisory referendum to vote on banning partisan gerrymandering. According to polls, the advisory referendum would pass the two-thirds threshold and justify bypassing the filibuster. If the President vetoes the bill to schedule the advisory referendum or the bill that bans partisan gerrymandering, Democrats could promise to pass the legislation again when a Democrat sits in the Oval Office.

Once signed into law, this book predicts that the Supreme Court will let it stand because the Court appears to be saying that it would enforce a law banning partisan gerrymandering should one exist.

Presidents are Not Above the Law

In July 2024, the Supreme Court ruled that the Constitution is unconstitutional. Article II, Section 4 states that the President, Vice President, and all civil officers of the United States "shall be removed from Office on Impeachment and Conviction of Treason, Bribery, or other high Crimes and Misdemeanors." However, the Supreme Court ruled 6 to 3 along partisan lines in *Trump v. United States* that the President "may not be prosecuted for exercising [their] core constitutional powers, and [are] entitled to at least presumptive immunity from prosecution for [their] official acts."[167]

Chief Justice Roberts justified the ruling by saying that the real problem is the "more likely prospect of an executive branch that cannibalizes itself, with each successive president free to prosecute his predecessors, yet unable to boldly and fearlessly carry out his duties for fear that he may be next."[168]

The ruling came less than two months after then former President Trump was found guilty in a Manhattan court on thirty-four felony counts of falsifying business records to hide a hush money payment to a porn star. This book asserts that falsifying business records to conceal hush money payments to a consenting adult should not be a felony. Worse for Democrats, the trial appeared to be politically motivated, which energized Trump supporters.

The Supreme Court's immunity ruling appears to have legalized bribery, extortion, and other crimes committed by the President. In President Trump's second term, corporations, wealthy individuals, and foreign governments have offered cash and expensive gifts for favors. Corruption in America is reminiscent of the Gilded Age, a period when suitcases full of cash and company stock certificates were delivered to lawmakers in exchange for favors.[169]

Neither the founding fathers nor current American voters want the leader of America to be a king. Polls have indicated that 70 percent of Americans oppose immunity for the President. This book recommends that Congressional Democrats draft a bill that removes immunity from the President. The bill should state that the Exceptions Clause will be invoked, and that lawsuits regarding Presidential crimes will be appealed to an anti-corruption court like the one described in chapter 1. If Senate Republicans filibuster the bill, Democrats could draft a bill scheduling an advisory referendum and send it to President Trump.

There is roughly a 100 percent chance that President Trump vetoes any bill that threatens Presidential immunity. In that event, Democrats could promise to pass the same bill when a Democrat sits in the White House. Who knows? The threat of loss of immunity might motivate President Trump to become more law-abiding, or not.

Eliminate the Electoral College

In 2000 and 2016, the winner of the U.S. presidential election did not win the most votes, but secured the presidency because of the electoral college. In 2025, five of the nine Supreme Court justices were nominated by those two presidents. None of the fifty states uses an electoral college, and no other country in the world uses an electoral college.[170]

America's president is elected by 538 electors who are chosen at the state level. Each state gets one elector for each of its Senators, and one elector for each member of the House of Representatives (Washington, D.C. gets three electors). Each political party puts up a slate of electors, and when voting for the president, voters are voting for a slate of electors. In all but two states, all electors come from the party that wins the state's vote for president. In Nebraska and Maine, some electors are chosen by separate voters in the U.S. House districts. In

December of an election year, the electors meet in their respective state capitals and cast their votes.[171]

To be elected, a presidential candidate must win a majority of the electoral votes, at least 270. If no candidate receives a majority, the House of Representatives chooses from among the top three candidates. Each state delegation in the House gets one vote, so the candidate with twenty-six or more votes becomes president. A state's House delegation does not have to support the candidate that won in their state. Thomas Jefferson and John Quincy Adams were elected by the House of Representatives.[172]

The main problem with the electoral college is that it can and has violated a fundamental rule of democratic elections—majority rule. The electoral college grants voters in small-population states more voting power than those in large states because small states get a minimum of three electoral votes (two for their Senators and one for their Representative) no matter how small their population. Because most smaller states vote Republican, it is estimated that Republicans have a twenty-vote advantage in the electoral college. Another problem is the winner-take-all arrangement in most states. This enables the winning candidate to receive all the state's electoral votes regardless of the margin of victory.[173]

From a campaign strategy perspective, presidential candidates only pay attention to voters in swing states. In 2020, 96 percent of the general-election campaign events were held in the twelve states where polling showed the candidates between 46 percent and 54 percent.[174]

The electoral college could be eliminated without an amendment. Article II of the Constitution gives states exclusive control over the method they use to award their electoral votes. The National Public Vote initiative is an effort to encourage states to pass laws that award their electoral votes to the presidential candidate who wins the most votes. By 2024, sixteen states and the District of Columbia had passed National Public Vote laws. These jurisdictions represent 205 electoral votes. Unfortunately, several swing states, including Pennsylvania, Michigan, Wisconsin, Georgia, Arizona, and Nevada, have not yet passed national voting laws.[175]

When states and jurisdictions representing 270 of the 538 electoral votes have passed National Popular Vote laws, the candidate receiving the most popular votes is guaranteed to win the presidential election.

Sixty-five percent of Americans want the popular vote, not the electoral college, to decide who is President. Democrats could encourage states to pass the National Public Vote initiative.

Advancing Democracy

America's democracy is in decline. Enacting the laws described above will advance democracy by prohibiting racial discrimination in voting, outlawing partisan gerrymandering, restoring the rule of law to the Presidency, and electing the President with a national vote instead of the outdated and undemocratic electoral college.

Chapter 6

Project 2027 New Rules

Project 2027's quality-of-life platform contains twelve laws in three categories: (1) restore women's reproductive rights and restrict election spending, (2) alleviate the hardship of nearly 200 hundred million Americans living paycheck to paycheck by reducing healthcare costs, reducing housing costs, and raising the minimum wage, and (3) advance democracy by restoring the Voting Rights Act, outlawing partisan gerrymandering, and eliminating presidential immunity and the electoral college.

All these policies have overwhelming voter support. However, all twelve laws can be blocked by the filibuster, and the Supreme Court stands ready to overturn at least three.

This chapter describes how the filibuster and the Supreme Court currently operate and how Democrats can start improving the quality of life in 2027.

The Filibuster and Its Rules

The United States Senate requires a simple majority of fifty-one votes to pass a bill after debate has ended. However, according to Senate rules, Senators who oppose a bill can extend debate by using a filibuster, and sixty votes are required to end a filibuster, as noted. Before the early 1970s, Senators had to stand and talk to filibuster. Since then, opposing Senators have been able to use a "silent" filibuster, meaning a bill can be blocked at any time if forty-one Senators threaten to filibuster.[176] The "silent" filibuster has made it easier for the minority party to block bills and appointments.

The purpose of the filibuster is to promote deliberation, thoughtful debate, and compromise. Since the 1990s, however, its use as an obstruction tool has increased as politics has become more partisan.[177]

Filibuster rules can be changed by a two-thirds vote in the Senate. The Congressional Budget Act of 1974, which the Senate passed unanimously, allows budget reconciliation to be exempt from the filibuster.[178] However, the Senate majority leader can also make exceptions to the filibuster on classes of bills and appointments with a simple majority vote.[179]

In recent years, Senate majority leaders have changed filibuster rules to stop obstruction. In 2008, Barack Obama and the Democrats swept into office, controlling the Presidency and both Houses of Congress for the first time since 1994. Obama promised a progressive agenda, and Republicans promised to obstruct everything President Obama tried to do. In 2013, after

Project 2027 New Rules

Senate Republicans repeatedly used the filibuster to block President Obama's cabinet and federal judge nominations, Senate Democrats, led by Senate Majority Leader Harry Reid, abolished the filibuster for most presidential appointments, except for those of Supreme Court Justices.[180] In 2017, Senate Republicans, led by Mitch McConnell, ended the filibuster on Supreme Court Justices, as noted.

The Republicans have become very good at obstruction. Against Obama, House and Senate Republicans repeatedly vowed to shut down the government unless President Obama repealed Obamacare and reduced federal spending, even though the unemployment rate was over nine percent. In August 2011, Obama reluctantly signed the Budget Control Act that raised the debt ceiling, thus preventing the government from defaulting, but also included spending and deficit reduction actions. A few days later, Standard & Poor's reduced the credit rating of the United States from AAA to AA+, the first time the U.S. credit rating had fallen below AAA since 1941.[181] In 2013, Republicans partially shut down the government for sixteen days.

The Republican's ability to block Obama's agenda crippled the economic recovery. Over six years were required for American workers to regain the jobs lost during the financial crisis, unemployment remained higher than it was before the fall of 2008, median wages remained flat, and an opioid epidemic raged through economically depressed communities.[182]

Although obstructing Obama was bad for Americans, it was good for Republicans. They won back the House of Representatives in 2010, the Senate in 2014, and the Presidency in 2016.[183]

In 2021, with Democrats again in control of the Presidency and both Houses of Congress, Democrats lacked the votes to overcome a Republican filibuster on bills that would have increased the minimum wage, restored the Voting Rights Act, and outlawed partisan gerrymandering, as noted.

Since 2017, the Senate has confirmed four Supreme Court justices with lifetime appointments with a simple majority vote. Since 2017, the Congressional Budget Act of 1974 has been used twice by the Senate to pass bills that cut taxes for corporations and the wealthiest Americans with a simple majority vote.[184] However, since 2009 the minimum wage has been stuck at $7.25 per hour because raising the minimum wage to help the poorest Americans requires a sixty-vote supermajority to overcome the Senate filibuster.

A Different Kind of Conservative Supreme Court

With the confirmation of Amy Coney Barrett in October 2020, Republican-appointed Justices held a 6 to 3 majority on the Supreme Court. Less than two years later, *Roe* was overturned. The 1973 Supreme Court that ruled 7 to 2 in *Roe v. Wade* also contained six Justices nominated by Republican Presidents.[185] Five of the six voted in favor of women's reproductive rights, and the decision was written by a Republican-appointed Justice. The majority ruled that the right to privacy implied in the 14th Amendment protected abortion as a fundamental right.[186]

In 2025, three of the six Republican-appointed Justices, Clarence Thomas, Neil Gorsuch, and Barrett, describe themselves as originalists, and John Roberts, Samuel Alito, and Brett Kavanaugh often express their opinions in originalist terms. That's a six-to-three majority for originalists. Originalists are a different breed of conservative.[187]

Originalism is a theory for interpreting the Constitution and its amendments based on the original public meaning that they would have had at the time of their writing.[188] In many cases, originalism makes sense. Judges should understand the meaning of the Constitution and the Amendments before ruling. Judges need to know that the President must be thirty-five years old, a natural born citizen, have lived in the U.S. for at least fourteen years, and cannot be elected more than twice.

However, if the text in the Constitution or the relevant Amendments is ambiguous or does not directly address the case before the Court, originalist doctrine instructs judges to examine the laws, court rulings, and social norms at the time the Constitution was written or the relevant amendment was ratified to inform their rulings. Most importantly, precedents and consequences in modern-day life do not matter.[189] (This book predicts that most Americans would not enjoy returning to the laws, court rulings, and social norms of the 1780s, when the Constitution was written, or the 1860s, when the 14th Amendment was ratified.)

Antonin Scalia was the first originalist to join the Supreme Court when he was appointed in 1986. Clarence Thomas was the second to join the Supreme Court in 1991. With Scalia and Thomas, eight of nine Justices on the Court were nominated by Republican Presidents. Still, five of the eight Republican-nominated Justices voted to uphold but narrow *Roe* in *Planned Parenthood of Southeastern Pennsylvania v. Casey* in 1992.[190]

For years, originalists, including the outspoken Scalia, claimed that the *Roe* decision was wrong because they doubted that the men who wrote the 14th Amendment in 1868 intended the right to privacy to apply to women.[191]

Justice Samuel Alito's majority opinion in *Dobbs* demonstrates how originalism can be applied when the text of the Constitution and the Amendments does not directly address the case before the Court. Alito correctly noted that the right to privacy for women is not explicitly stated in the Constitution or the Amendments. The words "women's reproductive rights" and "abortion" are also not found in the Constitution or the Amendments. Because these words are absent, originalists reason that women's reproductive rights would need to be deeply rooted in the nation's history, and the six Republican-nominated justices ruled that forty-nine years is not long enough.[192] Case closed. What doesn't matter: the 19th amendment that secured women's right to vote, the 1964 Civil

Rights Act that made employment discrimination against women illegal, multiple Supreme Court rulings that were based upon women's right to privacy, the fact that nothing had changed that could justify overturning *Roe* and *Casey* precedent, and the consequences to women's lives. The Dobbs ruling also contradicted the will of the people, including over half of Catholics.[193]

Originalist Justices Scalia and Thomas also joined the majority that ruled that corporations have First Amendment free-speech rights in *Citizens United*. The originalist justices claimed that *Citizens United* was true to originalist doctrine. However, scholars have gone to great lengths to cite irrefutable evidence that the *Citizens United* ruling violated originalism.[194] In the Court's *Trump v. United States* immunity ruling, the court appeared to have abandoned originalism altogether.[195] These criticisms miss the point.

The point is not that originalist justices are inconsistent or even hypocritical in their rulings. In *"Taking Back the Constitution: Activist Judges and the Next Age of American Law,"* author Mark Tushnet summed up originalism. He wrote, "originalism is a theory of judicial activism ... to stop liberals from achieving their legislative goals while not interfering with conservatives' favored laws."[196]

The tragedy is that under the cover of originalism, a conservative activist Supreme Court has made rulings that have damaged the quality of life, fueled division, and contradicted the will of the people.

New Day, New Rules

This book presents three moral, legal, and constitutional principles that can be used to bypass the Senate filibuster and the Supreme Court's judicial review under certain circumstances. These principles will allow Congress to enact legislation that improves the quality of life, advances democracy, unites America, and restores trust in government, with voters' overwhelming support.

1. Bills that schedule advisory referendums are not subject to Senate filibusters.
2. Bills that pass the two-thirds threshold in advisory referendums are not subject to Senate filibusters.
3. The Exceptions Clause can be used to remove judicial review from federal courts, including the Supreme Court, if the law in question advances democracy (e.g. promotes human rights or the rule of law or eliminates corruption), the law does not conflict with what the Constitution and Amendments explicitly state, using the Exceptions Clause has passed the two-thirds threshold in an advisory referendum, and the Supreme Court has struck down the same or similar laws. Further, bills invoking the Exception Clause that have passed the two-thirds threshold in an advisory referendum are not subject to Senate filibusters.

Once in control of Congress in 2027, Democrats can establish these new filibuster rules in the Senate with simple majority votes, schedule advisory referendums as necessary, and pass bills that improve the quality of life and advance democracy.

President Trump may sign some of these bills. He has talked about lowering prescription drug costs. The three laws described in chapter 2 would lower healthcare costs by nearly a one trillion dollars per year by 2032. He has also promised Americans high-paying jobs. Raising the minimum wage would increase wages for millions of Americans. However, if he vetoes any of these bills, Democrats could promise to pass the legislation again when a Democrat sits in the Oval Office.

Chapter 7

2029 and Beyond

As he was leaving the White House, Harry Truman said that America's middle class is what makes America the greatest country the sun has ever shone upon, or will ever shine upon (the middle class defined as having enough money to support yourself and your family without living hand to mouth). Between the 1930s and 1960s, policies passed by Democrats, including minimum wage laws, Social Security, home ownership laws, Medicare, and civil rights laws, along with government investments in education, medicine, defense, transportation, and science lifted tens of millions of Americans out of poverty.[197] America was the land of prosperity.

Because Democrats passed legislation that improved the quality of American life, they won most elections. Between 1932 and 1964, Democrats won the White House seven times in nine elections. From 1933 to 1981, Democrats held the Senate for forty-four of forty-eight years. From 1933 to 1995, Democrats held the House of Representatives for fifty-eight of sixty-two years. Democrats lost both houses of Congress just twice in sixty-two years.[198] [199]

This approach has worked recently for Colorado Democrats. Between 1972 and 2004, the Republican presidential candidate won the Colorado vote in eight of nine elections.[200] Beginning in 2008, the Democratic presidential candidate has won the Colorado vote in five consecutive elections. Before 2004, Democrats had not controlled both houses of the state legislature in four decades. From 2004 to 2024, Democrats have won both houses of the state legislature in eight of eleven elections.[201] Since 2007, a Democrat has been governor. Colorado Democrats continue to win because they focus on quality of life and pocketbook issues. (The next chapter describes how they did it.)

Rebuild Quality of Life

Today, nearly 200 million Americans live paycheck to paycheck because the cost of living has increased faster than income; 23 million women of reproductive age live in states with abortion bans; democracy has been compromised; and Americans are divided.[202] America needs the Democrats to deliver prosperity and reunite America.

This book predicts that this quality-of-life platform will secure both houses of Congress in 2026 and win the Presidency while retaining both houses of Congress in 2028, as noted.

2029 and Beyond

Democrats may even secure a filibuster-proof, sixty-seat majority in the Senate in 2028, making 2029 the year Democrats quickly and significantly improve the quality of life for millions of Americans.

History has shown that when Democrats pass laws that improve the quality of life, they win elections.

Let's make this happen.

Chapter 8

The Colorado Way

When the dust settled on the 2024 elections, there was a bright blue light: Colorado. Historically, Colorado was a state Republicans could count on in presidential elections and control of the state legislature. But Colorado turned blue in the 2000s and has stayed blue ever since. Here's how Colorado Democrats did it.

After losing most elections for decades, the Colorado Democratic party was in disarray. Further, the percentage of registered Democrats (30 percent) trailed the percentage of registered Republicans (36 percent) and unaffiliated voters (34 percent).

In 2003, four wealthy Democrats, Tim Gill, Rutt Bridges, Pat Stryker and Jared Polis came together to change Colorado's Democratic party. Later dubbed the "Gang of Four" by the press, Gill, Bridges, Stryker and Polis formed an alliance with Democrat-leaning groups called the "Roundtable."[203]

They took a business approach. They supported the most promising candidates across the state primarily based on polling. They didn't let policy disagreements or purity tests get in the way, which wasn't easy on hot-topic issues. They understood that for a political party to have power, it must be in power.[204]

Unlike state-level messaging used in the past, campaigns were surgical. The Democratic Roundtable used the Internet to identify individuals to target, such as independents, Republicans who didn't vote in the primary, and newcomers to the state. They distributed poll-tested, district-level messaging tailored to specific groups using mailings, radio, phone calls, and foot soldiers.

The strategy worked immediately. In 2004, Democrats won the state Senate and overcame a nine-seat deficit in the state House to reach a three-seat majority. It was the first time Democrats controlled both houses of the Colorado legislature in over forty years.[205]

In 2006, Democrats won the governor's mansion when Bill Ritter trounced his Republican opponent by nearly seventeen percentage points. Since then, Democrats have not lost a race for governor, and beginning in 2004, Democrats won the state Senate in nine of eleven elections and the state House in ten of eleven elections. In 2025, the governor and both U.S. senators

The Colorado Way

are Democrats, and Democrats are just a few seats shy of a supermajority in the state legislature.

Colorado Democrats keep winning because they pass laws that improve the quality of life in Colorado, and pocketbook issues are a priority. Colorado Democrats have reduced taxes, cut regulations, and reformed education.[206] [207]

The Democrat-led Denver School Board added charter schools and encouraged schools and teachers to innovate. Denver Public Schools improved from the bottom ten districts in the state on math and English/language arts performance to the top half of districts in the state.[208]

Governor Jared Polis promotes policies like universal pre-K, expanding light rail, and ending coal-burning for electricity generation as cost reductions, not moral imperatives. Colorado also has some of the strongest protections for women's and LGBTQ+ rights.[209]

Colorado Democrats may have another advantage. Colorado allows independents, or unaffiliated voters, to vote in either the Republican or the Democratic primary but not both. In an age of partisan politics, these "open" primaries tend to produce more moderate nominees. Open primaries may also help Democrats. It appears that Colorado Republicans think so. In 2023, the Colorado Republican Party sued the state to close its primary elections so that unaffiliated voters could not vote. A federal district judge ruled against the Republican party, and Colorado's primaries remain open to independents.[210]

The Colorado Way

National groups have begun to take notice. In April 2025, the Progressive Policy Institute convened in Colorado for its first gathering since the 2024 election. Will Marshall, president and founder, said, "We tried moving to the left under Biden. ... It really helped shrink the party's appeal."[211]

A pragmatic approach focusing on quality of life and pocketbook issues has worked for Colorado Democrats. It could work in other states and the national party too.

About the Author

Ed Minnock worked for eight companies, including six technology companies, three of which were rough-and-tumble startups. At startups, Ed learned how to assemble and lead teams that drive product development success.

When Ed joined Hewlett-Packard (HP) in 1992, he applied what he had learned to turn around HP's scanner and digital camera businesses. The scanner business won the President's Quality Award for HP's most outstanding business. The digital camera business became HP's fastest growing business. In 2002, Ed was promoted to vice president and general manager, responsible for two businesses with a combined revenue of $900 million.

After leaving HP, Ed worked for a consulting firm that taught companies how to use structured problem-solving to resolve their most difficult problems. Steps: (1) analyze the problem and its causes, (2) evaluate lots of alternatives, and (3) when a solution is found that meets or exceeds the goals, "Turn and burn." His clients included: Intel (U.S., Israel, Malaysia), Texas Instruments, Bombardier Aerospace (Canada), Kongsberg Automotive (Sweden and Norway), Fisher and

About the Author

Paykel (New Zealand), and Sara Lee (Indonesia, Malaysia) among others.

Ed then taught Business Ethics at Colorado State University's (CSU) College of Business. While teaching, he published *Teams vs. Plunderers*. He is a guest lecturer at CSU's College of Business and College of Engineering.

Ed earned a Master of Business Administration degree from Colorado State University and a Bachelor of Science degree in Operations Research / Industrial Engineering from Cornell University.

Ed and his family live in Fort Collins, Colorado.

Bibliography

Andersen, Kurt. *Evil Geniuses: The Unmaking of America: A Recent History.* Randon House, 2020.

Bair, Sheila. *Bull by the Horns: Fighting to Save Main Street from Wall Street and Wall Street from Itself.* Free Press, 2012.

Desmond, Matthew. *Poverty by America.* Crown, 2023.

Hughes, Chris. *Marketcrafters: The 100-Year Struggle to Shape the American Economy.* Avid Reader Press / Simon & Schuster, 2025.

Kaiser, Robert G. *So Damn Much Money: The Triumph of Lobbying and the Corrosion of American Government,* Knopf Doubleday Publishing Group, 2010.

Klein, Ezra, and Derek Thompson. *Abundance.* Avid Reader Press / Simon & Schuster, 2025.

Krugman, Paul. *Arguing with Zombies: Economics, Politics, and the Fight for a Better Future.* W. W. Norton & Company, 2020.

Levitsky, Steven, and Daniel Ziblatt. *Tyranny of the Minority: Why American Democracy Reached the Breaking Point.* Crown, 2023.

Matsusaka, John G. *Let the People Rule: How Direct Democracy Can Meet the Populist Challenge.* Princeton University Press, 2020.

McLean, Bethany, and Joe Nocera. *All the Devils Are Here: The Hidden History of the Financial Crisis.* Portfolio, 2011.

Bibliography

Meacham, Jon. *The Soul of America: The Battle for Our Better Angels.* Random House, 2018.

Mayer, Jane. *Dark Money: The Hidden History of the Billionaires Behind the Rise of the Radical Right.* Doubleday, 2016.

Reich, Robert. *Saving Capitalism: For the Many, Not the Few.* Knopf, 2015.

—. *The System: Who Rigged It, How We Fix It.* Knopf, 2020.

Schrager, Adam, Witwer, Rob. *The Blueprint: How the Democrats Won Colorado (and Why Republicans Everywhere Should Care).* Fulcrum Publishing, 2010.

Sorkin, Andrew Ross. *Too Big to Fail: The Inside Story of How Wall Street and Washington Fought to Save the Financial System—and Themselves.* Viking, 2009.

Teachout, Zephyr. *Corruption in America: From Benjamin Franklin's Snuff Box to Citizens United.* Harvard University Press, 2014.

Teixeira, Ruy, and Judis, John B. *Where Have All the Democrats Gone?: The Soul of the Party in the Age of Extremes.* Henry Holt and Co., 2023.

Tushnet, Mark. *Taking Back the Constitution: Activist Judges and the Next Age of American Law.* Yale University Press, 2020.

Winkler, Adam. *We the Corporations: How American Businesses Won Their Civil Rights.* Liveright, 2018.

End Notes

1. German Lopez, "America Leads the World in Drug Overdose Deaths—by a Lot," *Vox*, June 28, 2017, https://www.vox.com/policy-and-politics/2017/6/28/15881246/drug-overdose-deaths-world.

2. "Homelessness by Country 2024," *World Population Review*, accessed February 22, 2024, https://worldpopulationreview.com/country-rankings/homelessness-by-country.

3. "Confronting Poverty: Tools for Understanding Economic Hardship and Risk," accessed February 22, 2024, https://confrontingpoverty.org/poverty-facts-and-myths/americas-poor-are-worse-off-than-elsewhere/.

4. Annalisa Merelli, "The US Has a Lot of Money, but It Does Not Look Like a Developed Country," *Quartz*, March 10, 2017, https://qz.com/879092/the-us-doesnt-look-like-a-developed-country/.

5. Devon Haynie, "Report: American Quality of Life Declines Over Past Decade," *USNews*, September 11, 2020, https://www.usnews.com/news/best-countries/articles/2020-09-11/a-global-anomaly-the-us-declines-in-annual-quality-of-life-report.

6. Hannah Hartig, "Stark Partisan Divisions in Americans' Views of 'Socialism,' 'Capitalism'," *Pew Research Center*, June 25, 2019, https://www.pewresearch.org/short-reads/2019/06/25/stark-

End Notes

partisan-divisions-in-americans-views-of-socialism-capitalism/.

7   Ashely Balcerzak, "Study: Most Americans Want to Kill 'Citizens United' with Constitutional Amendment," *Center for Public Integrity*, May 10, 2018, https://publicintegrity.org/politics/study-most-americans-want-to-kill-citizens-united-with-constitutional-amendment/.

8   Emma Wager, Cynthia Cox, and Krutika Amin, "What Are the Recent and Forecasted Trends in Prescription Drug Spending," *Health System Tracker,* September 15, 2023, https://www.healthsystemtracker.org/chart-collection/recent-forecasted-trends-prescription-drug-spending/#Total%20out-of-pocket%20retail%20prescription%20drug%20spending,%20projections%20before%20&%20after%20passage%20of%20the%20Inflation%20Reduction%20Act.

9   David M. Dworkin and Dennis C. Shea, "Across the Aisle, Americans Look to Congress to Address Housing," *Newsweek,* June 25, 2024, https://www.newsweek.com/across-aisle-americans-look-congress-address-housing-opinion-1915898.

10   Erica Socker, "New Poll: Majority of Voters Want Congress to Take Action to Lower Health Care Prices," *Arnold Ventures*, June 30, 2021, https://www.arnoldventures.org/stories/new-poll-majority-of-voters-want-congress-to-take-action-to-lower-health-care-prices.

11   Sharon Zhang, "74 Percent of Voters Support Raising Federal Minimum Wage to $20 an Hour," *Truthout,* May 30, 2023, https://truthout.org/articles/74-percent-of-voters-support-raising-federal-minimum-wage-to-20-an-hour/.

12   Sarah Fortinshy, "70 Percent in New Poll Reject Trump Presidential Immunity Claim," *The Hill,* Marh 18, 2024,

End Notes

https://thehill.com/regulation/court-battles/4538931-70-percent-reject-trump-presidential-immunity-claim/.

13   "Americans Are United Against Partisan Gerrymandering," *Brennan Center for Justice,* March 15, 2019, https://www.brennancenter.org/our-work/research-reports/americans-are-united-against-partisan-gerrymandering.

14   Jocelyn Kiley, "Majority of Americans Continue to Favor Moving Away from Electoral College," *Pew Research Center,* September 25, 2024, https://www.pewresearch.org/short-reads/2023/09/25/majority-of-americans-continue-to-favor-moving-away-from-electoral-college.

15   Alison Durkee, "How Americans Really Feel About Abortion: The Sometimes Surprising Poll Results One Year After Roe Overturned," *Forbes,* June 26, 2023, https://www.forbes.com/sites/alisondurkee/2023/06/26/how-americans-really-feel-about-abortion-the-sometimes-surprising-poll-results-one-year-after-roe-overturned/?sh=5455ee7b5ea3.

16   Steven Levitsky and Daniel Ziblatt, *Tyranny of the Minority* (Random House, 2023).

17   Adam Winkler, *We the Corporations: How American Businesses Won Their Civil Rights* (Liveright, 2018).

18   "Roe v. Wade and Supreme Court Abortion Cases," *Brennan Center for Justice,* September 28, 2022, https://www.brennancenter.org/our-work/research-reports/roe-v-wade-and-supreme-court-abortion-cases#:~:text=justices'%20abortion%20views-,Is%20abortion%20a%20constitutional%20right%3F,a%20constitutional%20right%20to%20abortion.

19   Jolynn Dellinger and Stephanie K. Pell, "The Criminalization of

End Notes

Abortion and Surveillance of Women in a Post-Dobbs World," *Brookings*, April 18, 2024, https://www.brookings.edu/articles/the-criminalization-of-abortion-and-surveillance-of-women-in-a-post-dobbs-world/#:~:text=Georgia%20and%20Florida%20are%20just,the%20law%20of%20the%20land.

20. "Roe v. Wade and Supreme Court Abortion Cases," *Brennan Center for Justice*, see note 18.

21. Leo E. Strine Jr. and Nicholas Walter, "Originalist or Original: The Difficulties of Reconciling *Citizens United* with Corporate Law History," *Notre Dame Law Review*, April 2016, https://scholarship.law.nd.edu/ndlr/vol91/iss3/1/.

22. Pam Belluck, "The History Behind Arizona's 160-Year-Old Abortion Ban," *New York Times*, April 10, 2024, https://www.nytimes.com/2024/04/10/health/arizona-abortion-ban-history.html.

23. "State Bans on Abortion Throughout Pregnancy," *Guttmacher*, March 26, 2025, https://www.guttmacher.org/state-policy/explore/state-policies-abortion-bans#:~:text=12%20states%20have%20a%20total,some%20point%20after%2018%20weeks.

24. Deepa Shivaram, "A Bill to Codify Abortion Protections Fails in the Senate," *NPR*, May 11, 2024, https://www.npr.org/2022/05/11/1097980529/senate-to-vote-on-a-bill-that-codifies-abortion-protections-but-it-will-likely-f.

25. Paul Dans and Steve Groves, *Project 2025: Mandate for Leadership, The Conservative Promise*. (The Heritage Foundation, 2023).

26. John G. Matsusaka, *Let the People Rule: How Direct Democracy Can Meet the Populist Challenge*. (Princeton University Press,

End Notes

2020).

[27] Shane Harrison, "Irish Abortion Referendum: Ireland Overturns Abortion Ban," *BBC*, May 26, 2018, https://www.bbc.com/news/world-europe-44256152.

[28] Matsusaka, *Let the People Rule*, see note 26.

[29] Ibid.

[30] Richard Alber, "The World's Most Difficult Constitution to Amend," *California Law Review*, December, 2022, https://www.californialawreview.org/print/the-worlds-most-difficult-constitution-to-amend.

[31] Matsusaka, *Let the People Rule*, see note 26.

[32] "An Examination of the 2016 Electorate, Based on Validated Voters," *Pew Research Center*, August 9, 2018, https://www.pewresearch.org/politics/2018/08/09/an-examination-of-the-2016-electorate-based-on-validated-voters/.

[33] "Behind Biden's 2020 Victory," *Pew Research Center*, August 30, 2021, https://www.pewresearch.org/politics/2021/06/30/behind-bidens-2020-victory/.

[34] "The Legislative Process," *Congress.gov*, accessed May 24, 2025 https://www.congress.gov/legislative-process/presidential-action#:~:text=Presidential%20Actions%20(Transcript)&text=If%20the%20bill%20is%20signed,has%20adjourned%20under%20certain%20circumstances).

[35] Carl Hulse, "How Mitch McConnell Delivered Justice Amy Coney Barrett's Rapid Confirmation," *New York Times*, April 10, 2020, https://www.nytimes.com/2020/10/27/us/mcconnell-barrett-

End Notes

confirmation.html.

36 "Federal Human Rights Laws," *Office of Human Rights*, accessed March 27, 2025, https://ohr.dc.gov/page/federal-human-rights-laws.

37 Brian Kulp, "Counteracting Marbury: Using The Exceptions Clause to Overrule Supreme Court Precedent," *Harvard University*, January 2020, https://journals.law.harvard.edu/jlpp/wp-content/uploads/sites/90/2020/01/Kulp-FINAL.pdf.

38 "ArtIII.S1.8.6 Courts of Specialized Jurisdiction and Congress," *Congress.gov*, accessed March 27, 2025, https://constitution.congress.gov/browse/essay/artIII-S1-8-6/ALDE_00013562/.

39 "Judgeship Reassignments," *Federal Judicial Center*, accessed March 27, 2025, https://www.fjc.gov/history/judges/judgeship-reassignments#:~:text=As%20part%20of%20its%20power,altered%20them%20in%20other%20ways.

40 Adam Winkler, *We the Corporations: How American Businesses Won Their Civil Rights* (Liveright, 2018).

41 *McCutcheon, et al. v. FEC, Federal Election Commission*, accessed March 27, 2025, https://www.fec.gov/legal-resources/court-cases/mccutcheon-et-al-v-fec/.

42 "Stephen Colbert's Super PAC Lessons," *NBC News*, accessed March 20, 2024, https://www.youtube.com/watch?v=oy7TUtlPmqk.

43 "Jon Stewart to Oversee Stephen Colbert SuperPAC," *ABC News*, accessed March 20, 2024, https://www.youtube.com/watch?v=AuqSELPyNSo.

44 Saurav Ghosh, "PACs, Super PACs and More: Your Guide to Key

End Notes

Election Spending Vehicles," *Campaign Legal Center*, September 15, 2022, https://campaignlegal.org/update/pacs-super-pacs-and-more-your-guide-key-election-spending-vehicles.

45 Kenneth P. Vogel and Shane Goldmacher, "An Unusual $1.6 Billion Donation Bolsters Conservatives," *New York Times*, August 22, 2022, https://www.nytimes.com/2022/08/22/us/politics/republican-dark-money.html.

46 David Luhnow, "It's Costly, Long and Exhausting: Welcome to America's Elections," *Wall Street Journal*, October 26, 2024, https://www.wsj.com/politics/elections/elections-cost-us-highest-spend-b8475961.

47 "Who Are the Biggest Donors?," *Open Secrets*, accessed March 27, 2025, https://www.opensecrets.org/elections-overview/biggest-donors.

48 "Lobbying Data Summary," *Open Secrets*, accessed March 27, 2025, https://www.opensecrets.org/federal-lobbying.

49 Robert Kaiser, *So Damn Much Money: The Triumph of Lobbying and the Corrosion of American Government.* (Knopf Doubleday Publishing Group, 2010).

50 Robert Reich, *The System: Who Rigged It, How We Fix It* (Alfred A. Knopf, 2020).

51 Craig Holman, "Corporations and Billionaires Flooded Trump's Inauguration with Cash," *Otherwords*, January 22, 2025, https://otherwords.org/corporations-and-billionaires-flooded-trumps-inauguration-with-cash/.

52 Rebecca Ballhaus, Dana Mattioli, and Annie Linskey, "How the Trumps Turned an Election Victory Into a Cash Bonanza," *Wall*

End Notes

Street Journal, February 13, 2025, https://www.wsj.com/politics/elections/trump-family-election-cash-bonanza-2f5f8714.

53 Robert Reich, *Saving Capitalism: For the Many, Not the Few* (Alfred A. Knopf, 2015).

54 Kavita K. Patel and Kevin A. Schulman, "Policy Options to Reduce Prescription Drug Costs Across Medicare, Medicaid, and Commercial Insurance," *Stanford Medicine, Department of Medicine News*, accessed March 27, 2025, https://medicine.stanford.edu/news/current-news/standard-news/policy-options-white-paper.html#:~:text=While%20cost%2Dsavings%20in%20Medicare,market%20more%20transparent%20and%20accessible.

55 David U. Himmelstein, Robert M. Lawless, Deborah Thorne, Pamela Foohey, and Steffie Woolhandler, "Medical Bankruptcy: Still Common Despite the Affordable Care Act," *NIH: National Library of Medicine*, March 2019, https://pmc.ncbi.nlm.nih.gov/articles/PMC6366487/#:~:text=The%20majority%20(58.5%25)%20%E2%80%9Cvery,530%20000%20medical%20bankruptcies%20annually.

56 Reich, *The System*, see note 50.

57 Clara Haverstic, "57% of Americans Live Paycheck to Paycheck in 2025, MarketWatch, May 14, 2025, https://www.marketwatch.com/financial-guides/banking/paycheck-to-paycheck-statistics/.

58 Reich, *The System*, see note 50.

End Notes

59 "Corruption Perceptions Index," *Transparency International*, accessed March 25, 2024, https://www.transparency.org/en/cpi/2021/index/usa.

60 Matsusaka, *Let the People Rule*, see note 26.

61 Jenny Anderson, "The Three Things That Make British Elections So Different from American Ones," *Institute for Government*, November 7, 2019, https://www.instituteforgovernment.org.uk/explainer/election-spending-regulated-uk.

62 Michael Pinto-Duschinsky, Alexander Postnikov, "Campaign Finance in Foreign Countries: Legal Regulation and Political Practices (A Comparative Legal Survey and Analysis)," International Foundation for Election Systems, February 1999, https://www.ifes.org/sites/default/files/migrate/campaign_finance.pdf.

63 Zephyr Teachout, *Corruption in America: From Benjamin Franklin's Snuff Box to Citizens United* (Harvard University Press, 2014).

64 "Receiving a public funding grant for the general election," *Federal Election Commission*, accessed October 3, 2024, https://www.fec.gov/help-candidates-and-committees/understanding-public-funding-presidential-elections/receiving-public-funding-grant-for-general-election/.

65 Renu Zaretsky, "What's to Become of the Presidential Election Campaign Fund?," *Tax Policy Center*, June 5, 2024, https://taxpolicycenter.org/taxvox/whats-become-presidential-election-campaign-fund,

66 Matsusaka, *Let the People Rule*, see note 26.

End Notes

67   Levitsky and Ziblatt, *Tyranny of the Minority*, see note 16.

68   Kelly, Martin, "Why the Articles of Confederation Failed," *Thought Co.*, https://www.thoughtco.com/why-articles-of-confederation-failed-104674, May 8, 2020

69   Matsusaka, *Let the People Rule*, see note 26.

70   "Receiving a public funding grant for the general election," see note 64.

71   Douglass J. Amy, "The Immense and Disturbing Power of Judicial Review," *Second-Rate Democracy*, accessed April 27, 2025, https://secondratedemocracy.com/the-problem-of-judicial-review/.

72   Carsten Smith, "Judicial review of parliamentary legislation: Norway as a European pioneer," *Amicus Curiae*, https://scispace.com/pdf/judicial-review-of-parliamentary-legislation-norway-as-a-3ilvaxb2tk.pdf.

73   Levitsky and Ziblatt, *Tyranny of the Minority*, see note 16.

74   Max Baucus and Kenneth R. Kay, "The Court Stripping Bills: Their Impact on the Constitution, the Courts, and Congress," *Villanova Law Review 27, n.5 (1982)*, https://digitalcommons.law.villanova.edu/cgi/viewcontent.cgi?article=2375&context=vlr.

75   Kia Rahnama, "The Other Tool Democrats Have to Rein in the Supreme Court," *Politico*, October 26, 2020, https://www.politico.com/news/magazine/2020/10/26/amy-coney-barrett-confirmation-court-packing-jursidiction-stripping-432566

76   "Mirror, Mirror 2021: Reflecting Poorly Health Care in the U.S. Compared to Other High-Income Countries," *The Commonwealth Fund*, August 4, 2021,

End Notes

https://www.commonwealthfund.org/publications/fund-reports/2021/aug/mirror-mirror-2021-reflecting-poorly.

77 Matthew McGough, Emma Wager, Aubrey Winger, Nirmita Pancal, and Lynne Cotter, "How Has U.S. Spending on Healthcare Changed Over Time?," *Peterson-KFF Health System Tracker*, December 20, 2024, https://www.healthsystemtracker.org/chart-collection/u-s-spending-healthcare-changed-time/#Total%20national%20health%20expenditures,%201970-2023

78 Juliette Cubanski, Alice Burns, and Cynthia Cox, "What Does the Federal Government Spend on Health Care?," *KFF*, February 24, 2025, https://www.kff.org/medicaid/issue-brief/what-does-the-federal-government-spend-on-health-care/.

79 Socker, "New Poll: Majority of Voters Want Congress to Take Action to Lower Health Care Prices," see note 10.

80 "CMS' program history," *CMS.Gov*, accessed April, 1, 2025, https://www.cms.gov/about-cms/who-we-are/history#:~:text=The%20Medicare%20Prescription%20Drug%20Improvement,went%20into%20effect%20in%202006.

81 Rahnama, "The Other Tool Democrats Have to Rein in the Supreme Court," see note 75.

82 Juliette Cubanski, Tricia Neuman, and Meredith Freed, "Explaining the Prescription Drug Provisions in the Inflation Reduction Act," *KFF*, January 24, 2023, https://www.kff.org/medicare/issue-brief/explaining-the-prescription-drug-provisions-in-the-inflation-reduction-act/#:~:text=The%20law%20that%20established%20the,require%20a%20particular%20formulary%20or.

83 Socker, "New Poll: Majority of Voters Want Congress to Take

End Notes

Action to Lower Health Care Prices," see note 10.

84 Rahnama, "The Other Tool Democrats Have to Rein in the Supreme Court," see note 75.

85 Cubanski, Neuman, and Freed, "Explaining the Prescription Drug Provisions in the Inflation Reduction Act," see note 82.

86 Alyce McFadden, "The long, costly battle over Obamacare might be over," *Open Secrets*, June 23, 2021, https://www.opensecrets.org/news/2021/06/costly-battle-obamacare-over/#:~:text=2009:%20Building%20Obamacare&text=The%20healthcare%20industry%20spent%20more,after%20the%20bill%20became%20law.

87 Glenn Greenwald, "Obamacare Architect Leaves White House for Pharmaceutical Industry Job," *The Guardian*, December 5, 2012, https://www.theguardian.com/commentisfree/2012/dec/05/obamacare-fowler-lobbyist-industry1.

88 McGough, Wager, Winger, Pancal, and Cotter, "How Has U.S. Spending on Healthcare Changed Over Time?," see note 77.

89 Sam Hughes, Emily Gee, and Nicole Rapfogel, "Health Insurance Costs Are Squeezing Workers and Employers," The Center for American Progress, November 29, 2022, https://www.americanprogress.org/article/health-insurance-costs-are-squeezing-workers-and-employers/.

90 Amy Skinner, "How Rising Healthcare Costs Have Caused Small Businesses to Eliminate Benefits," TakeCommand, accesses June 11, 2025, https://www.takecommandhealth.com/rising-healthcare-costs-small-

End Notes

business#:~:text=Rising%20healthcare%20costs%20have%20put,sponsored%20insurance%20at%20small%20firms.

91 "Ozempic for Weight Loss: Does It Work, and What Do Experts Recommend?," *UC Davis Health*, July 19, 2023, https://health.ucdavis.edu/blog/cultivating-health/ozempic-for-weight-loss-does-it-work-and-what-do-experts-recommend/2023/07.

92 Zarchary J. Ward, Walter C. Willett, Frank B. Hu, Lorena S. Pacheco, Michael W. Long, and Steven L. Gortmaker, "Excess Mortality Associated with Elevated Body Weight in the USA by State and Demographic Subgroup: A Modelling Study," *National Library of Medicine*, April 28, 2022, https://pmc.ncbi.nlm.nih.gov/articles/PMC9065308/#:~:text=Evidence%20before%20the%20study,associated%20with%20elevated%20body%20weight.

93 "Ozempic for Weight Loss," *UC Davis Health*, see note 91.

94 Krutika Amin, Imani Telesford, Rakesh Singh, and Cynthia Cox, "How do Prices of Drugs for Weight Loss in the U.S. Compare to Peer Nations' Prices?," *Peterson-KFF Health System Tracker*, August 17, 2023, https://www.healthsystemtracker.org/brief/prices-of-drugs-for-weight-loss-in-the-us-and-peer-nations/.

95 Patel and Schulman, "Policy Options to Reduce Prescription Drug Costs Across Medicare, Medicaid, and Commercial Insurance," see note 54.

96 Cubanski, Neuman, and Freed, "Explaining the Prescription Drug Provisions in the Inflation Reduction Act," see note 82.

97 Ibid.

End Notes

98 Merelli, "The US Has a Lot of Money, but It Does Not Look Like a Developed Country," see note 4.

99 "Medicare Drug Price Negotiation Program: Selected Drugs for Initial Price Applicability Year 2027," *CMS.Gov – Medicare Drug Price Negotiation Program*, January 2025, https://www.cms.gov/files/document/factsheet-medicare-negotiation-selected-drug-list-ipay-2027.pdf.

100 Hannah-Alise Rogers, "Constitutional Challenges to the Medicare Drug Price Negotiation," *Congress.gov*, October 10, 2024, https://www.congress.gov/crs-product/R47682.

101 Patel and Schulman, "Policy Options to Reduce Prescription Drug Costs Across Medicare, Medicaid, and Commercial Insurance," see note 54.

102 Ekaterian Galkina Cleary, Matthew Jackson, and Edward Zhou, "New Study Shows NIH Investment in New Drug Approvals Is Comparable to Investment by Pharmaceutical Industry," *Bentley University*, April 28, 2023, https://www.bentley.edu/news/new-study-shows-nih-investment-new-drug-approvals-comparable-investment-pharmaceutical#:~:text=Total%20NIH%20spending%20was%20$187%20billion%2C%20with,involving%20applied%20research%20on%20the%20drugs%20themselves.&text=Considering%20that%20NIH%2Dfunded%20research%20on%20a%20validated,of%20$711%20million%20per%20drug%20approved%202010%2D2019.

103 Matt Wirz, "Private Equity's Food Binge Goes Sour," *Wall Street Journal*, February 18, 2021, https://www.wsj.com/articles/private-equitys-food-binge-goes-sour-8f830dd4?gaa_at=eafs&gaa_n=ASWzDAjYiRe4SCFGboJ1X7c_tvCy-iBE--SigerotuMCoXyv10G8KImrYMaLxERZB9A%3D&gaa_ts=683a5e5

End Notes

5&gaa_sig=aPAoy0N7dTvceXwzPknM1KPsUUfyQuM51L-xDFdJ4kgT5hlrsS6Ff2e-08sUvIyqGXSjdVMOOimakjJqDxr9Ag%3D%3D.

[104] "Private Health Plans During 2022 Paid Hospitals 254 Percent of What Medicare Would Pay," *Rand*, accessed April 1, 2025, https://www.rand.org/news/press/2024/05/13.html#:~:text=Even%20as%20the%20number%20of,to%20254%20percent%20in%202022.

[105] Peter Goodman, *Davos Man: How the Billionaires Devoured the World* (Custom House, 2022).

[106] Wirz, "Private Equity's Food Binge Goes Sour," see note 103.

[107] Socker, "New Poll: Majority of Voters Want Congress to Take Action to Lower Health Care Prices," see note 10.

[108] Scott Zamost, "Inside the Mind of Criminals: How to Brazenly Steal $100 Billion from Medicare and Medicaid," *CNBC*, March 9, 2022, https://www.cnbc.com/2023/03/09/how-medicare-and-medicaid-fraud-became-a-100b-problem-for-the-us.html.

[109] Christopher Weaver, Tom McGinty, Anna Wilde Mathews, and Mark Maremount, "Insurers Pocketed $50 Billion From Medicare for Diseases No Doctor Treated," *Wall Street Journal*, July 8, 2024, https://www.wsj.com/health/healthcare/medicare-health-insurance-diagnosis-payments-b4d99a5d.

[110] Reed Abelson and Margot Sanger-Katz, "'The Cash Monster Was Insatiable': How Insurers Exploited Medicare for Billions," *New York Times*, October 8, 2022, https://www.nytimes.com/2022/10/08/upshot/medicare-advantage-fraud-allegations.html.

End Notes

[111] Zamost, "Inside the Mind of Criminals," see note 108.

[112] Bethany McLean and Joe Nocera, *All the Devils Are Here: The Hidden History of the Financial Crisis*, (Portfolio, 2011).

[113] Gregory Zuckerman, *The Greatest Trade Ever: The Behind-the-Scenes Story of How John Paulson Defied Wall Street and Made Financial History* (Crown, 2009).

[114] Colin McArthur and Sarah Edelman, "The 2008 Housing Crisis," *American Progress*, April 13, 2017, https://www.americanprogress.org/issues/economy/reports/2017/04/13/430424/2008-housing-crisis.

[115] McLean and Nocera, *All the Devils Are Here*, see note 112.

[116] Sheila Bair, *Bull by the Horns: Fighting to Save Main Street from Wall Street and Wall Street from Itself* (Free Press, 2012).

[117] McLean and Nocera, *All the Devils Are Here*, see note 112.

[118] Ibid.

[119] Paul Kiel and Olga Pierce, "Dems: Obama Broke Pledge to Force Banks to Help Homeowners," *ProPublica*, February 4, 2011, https://www.propublica.org/article/dems-obama-broke-pledge-to-force-banks-to-help-homeowners.

[120] Francesca Mari, "A $60 Billion Housing Grab by Wall Street," *New York Times*, October 22, 2021, https://www.nytimes.com/2020/03/04/magazine/wall-street-landlords.html.

[121] Valerie Stahl, "Welcome to Blackstone: How Private Equity Is Gobbling Up the American City and Turning Residents into Collateral," *Tablet*, July 4, 2023, https://www.tabletmag.com/sections/news/articles/welcome-

End Notes

blackstone-usa.

[122] Laurie Goodman, Amalie Zinn, Katherine Reynolds, and Owen Noble, "A Profile of Institutional Investor Owned Single-Family Rental Properties," *Housing Financial Policies Center – Urban Institute,* April 25, 2023, https://www.urban.org/sites/default/files/2023-04/A%20Profile%20of%20Institutional%20Investor%E2%80%93Owned%20Single-Family%20Rental%20Properties_0.pdf.

[123] McArthur and Edelman, "The 2008 Housing Crisis," see note 114.

[124] Ibid.

[125] Ibid.

[126] Ronda Kaysen, "New Legislation Proposes to Take Wall Street Out of the Housing Market," *New York Times,* December 3, 2023, https://www.nytimes.com/2023/12/06/realestate/wall-street-housing-market.html.

[127] "HM1.1. Housing Stock and Construction," *OECD Affordable Housing Database,* accessed April 3, 2025, https://www.oecd.org/content/dam/oecd/en/data/datasets/affordable-housing-database/hm1-1-housing-stock-and-construction.pdf.

[128] "How Long Does It Take to Save for a House," *WTF Happened in 1971,* accessed April 5, 2025, https://www.youtube.com/watch?app=desktop&v=auV3099wmPI.

[129] Ezra Klein and Derek Thompson, *Abundance* (Avid Reader Press / Simon & Schuster, 2025).

[130] Ibid.

[131] Laurel Rosenhall Soumya Karlamangla and Adam Nagourney, "California Rolls Back Its Landmark Environmental Law, *"New York

115

End Notes

Times, July 1, 2025, https://www.nytimes.com/2025/06/30/us/california-environment-newsom-ceqa.html

[132] "Since 1938 the Minimum Wage Has Been Increased "23 Times" and Was Raised "21 Times During Democratic Congresses, and Only Twice During Republican Ones"," *PolitiFact – The Poynter Institute,* February 11, 2019, https://www.politifact.com/factchecks/2019/feb/14/facebook-posts/yes-democrats-held-majority-almost-every-time-cong/.

[133] Greg Lacurci, "The $7.25 Minimum Wage Can't Pay All The Bills in Any State," *CNBC,* March 2, 2021, https://www.cnbc.com/2021/03/02/the-7point25-minimum-wage-doesnt-help-families-pay-the-bills-in-any-state.html.

[134] "The Walmart Tax Subsidy," *Americans for Tax Fairness,* April 2015, https://americansfortaxfairness.org/files/Taxpayers-and-Walmart-ATF.pdf.

[135] "2015 Walmart Annual Report," https://www.annualreports.com/HostedData/AnnualReportArchive/w/NYSE_WMT_2015_ddd82380ab80464280dda19c0e7d4379.pdf.

[136] Charles Fishman, *The Wal-Mart Effect: How the World's Most Powerful Company Really Works–and How It's Transforming the American Economy* (Penguin Books, 2006).

[137] Theron Mohamed, "The Walmart Heirs Are Worth $330 Billion. Sam Walton's Smart Move in the 1950s Is a Big Reason Why," *Yahoo Finance,* August 26, 2024, https://finance.yahoo.com/news/walmart-heirs-worth-330-billion-164602857.html.

[138] "The Walmart Tax Subsidy," *Americans for Tax Fairness,* see note

End Notes

134.

[139] Matthew Desmond, *Poverty by America* (Crown, 2023).

[140] Gavin Newsom, "Gavin Newsom: Critics Said California's Minimum Wage Increase Would Be a Job Killer. The Opposite Happened." *Fox News*, September 18, 2024, https://www.foxnews.com/opinion/gavin-newsom-critics-said-californias-minimum-wage-increase-would-job-killer-opposite-happened.

[141] Ashleigh Fields, "Democrats unveil legislation raising federal minimum wage to $17 an hour," *The Hill*, April 8, 2025, https://thehill.com/homenews/house/5238741-federal-minimum-wage-increase-bill/.

[142] John Myers, Johana Bhuiyan, and Margot Roosevelt, "Newsom Signs Bill Rewriting California Employment Law, Limiting Use of Independent Contractors," *Los Angeles Times*, September 18, 2019, https://www.latimes.com/california/story/2019-09-18/gavin-newsom-signs-ab5-employees0independent-contractors-california.

[143] Suhauna Hussain, Johana Bhuiyan, and Ryan Menezes, "How Uber and Lyft Persuaded California to Vote their Way," *Los Angeles Times*, November 13, 2020, https://www.latimes.com/business/technology/story/2020-11-13/how-uber-lyft-doordash-won-proposition-22.

[144] Curran McSwigan, "Explainer: Benefits Models for Gig Workers," *Third Way*, April 12, 2022, https://www.thirdway.org/report/explainer-benefits-models-for-gig-workers.

[145] Ibid.

[146] Faiz Siddiqui and Nitasha Tiku, "Uber and Lyft Used Sneaky

End Notes

Tactics to Avoid Making Drivers Employees in California, Voters Say. Now They're Going National." *Washington Post*, November 17, 2020, https://www.washingtonpost.com/technology/2020/11/17/uber-lyft-prop22-misinformation/.

147 Jonathan Gruber, "How Should We Provide Benefits to Gig Workers?," *Brookings*, June 13, 2024, https://www.brookings.edu/articles/how-should-we-provide-benefits-to-gig-workers/.

148 Brian Straight, "Conflicting Surveys Continue to Cloud the Picture on the Best Approach to Employment Status," *Freight Waves*, June 04, 2021, https://www.freightwaves.com/news/do-gig-workers-want-to-be-employees-it-depends-who-you-ask.

149 Desmond, *Poverty by America*, see note 139.

150 Rachel Kleinfield, "Five Strategies to Support U.S. Democracy," *Carnegie Endowment for International Peace*, September 15, 2022, https://carnegieendowment.org/2022/09/15/five-strategies-to-support-u.s.-democracy-pub-87918.

151 Levitsky and Ziblatt, *Tyranny of the Minority*, see note 16.

152 "Homelessness by Country 2024," *World Population Review*, see note 2.

153 "Confronting Poverty," see note 3.

154 Levitsky and Ziblatt, *Tyranny of the Minority*, see note 16.

155 Ibid.

156 Ibid.

End Notes

157. "Bipartisan Support for Early In-Person Voting, Voter ID, Election Day National Holiday," *Pew research Center*, February 7, 2024, https://www.pewresearch.org/politics/2024/02/07/bipartisan-support-for-early-in-person-voting-voter-id-election-day-national-holiday/.

158. Gruber, "How should We Provide Benefits to Gig Workers?," see note 147.

159. Levitsky and Ziblatt, *Tyranny of the Minority*, see note 16.

160. Ibid.

161. Paul Dillar, "Gerrymandering and Local Democracy," *Local Solutions Support Center*, August 2018, https://www.abetterbalance.org/wp-content/uploads/2018/10/Gerrymandering-White-Paper-FINAL-8.8.18.pdf.

162. "How the Supreme Court Made Racial Gerrymandering Easier in Alexander v. South Carolina NAACP," *League of Women Voters*, August 13, 2024, https://www.lwv.org/blog/how-supreme-court-made-racial-gerrymandering-easier-alexander-v-south-carolina-naacp.

163. Kleinfield, "Five Strategies to Support U.S. Democracy," see note 150.

164. Ibid.

165. "H.R. 1 – The For the People Act," *Committee on House Administration*, accessed April 19, 2025, https://democrats-cha.house.gov/hr-1-people-act.

166. Jacob Pramuk. "Senate Republicans block Democrats' sweeping voting, ethics bill," CNBC, June, 22, 2021, https://www.cnbc.com/2021/06/22/senate-to-vote-on-s1-for-the-

End Notes

people-act-bill.html

167 Thomas Wolf, "Supreme Court's Radical Immunity Ruling Shields Lawbreaking Presidents and Undermines Democracy," Brennan Center for Justice, July 2, 2024, https://www.brennancenter.org/our-work/analysis-opinion/supreme-courts-radical-immunity-ruling-shields-lawbreaking-presidents-and.

168 Dillar, "Gerrymandering and Local Democracy," see note 161.

169 "Corruption Perceptions Index," *Transparency International*, see note 59.

170 Douglass A. Amy, "The Electoral College: A Peculiar and Undemocratic Tradition," *Second-Rate Democracy*, 2020, https://secondratedemocracy.com/outmoded-electoral-college/.

171 "H.R. 1 – The For the People Act," *Committee on House Administration*, see note 165.

172 Ibid.

173 Ibid.

174 "Agreement Among the States to Elect the President by National Popular Vote," *National Popular Vote*, accessed March 29, 2024, https://www.nationalpopularvote.com/written-explanation.

175 "Status of National Popular Vote Bill in Each State," *National Popular Vote*, accessed October 4, 2024, https://www.nationalpopularvote.com/state-status.

176 Tim Lau, "The Filibuster Explained," *Brennan Venter for Justice*, April 26, 2021, https://www.brennancenter.org/our-work/research-reports/filibuster-explained#:~:text=As%20Senate%20gridlock%20persists%2C%20c

End Notes

alls,cabinet%20appointments%2C%20among%20other%20measures.

[177] Ibid.

[178] "H.R.7130 – Congressional Budget and Impoundment Control Act of 1974," *Congress.gov*, accessed May 25, 2025, https://www.congress.gov/bill/93rd-congress/house-bill/7130/all-actions?q=%7B%22roll-call-vote%22%3A%22S%22%7D.

[179] Lau, "The Filibuster Explained," see note 176.

[180] Jeremy Peters, "In Landmark Vote, Senate Limits Use of the Filibuster, *New York Times*, November 21, 2013, https://www.nytimes.com/2013/11/22/us/politics/reid-sets-in-motion-steps-to-limit-use-of-filibuster.html.

[181] Paul Krugman, *Arguing with Zombies: Economics, Politics, and the Fight for a Better Future* (W. W. Norton & Company, 2020)

[182] Chris Hughes, *Marketcrafters: The 100-Year Struggle to Shape the American Economy.* (Avid Reader Press / Simon & Schuster, 2025).

[183] "Here's What Happened the Last Time the Government Shut Down," *ABC News*, November 18, 2014, https://abcnews.go.com/Politics/heres-happened-time-government-shut/story?id=26997023.

[184] Richard Kogan and David Reich, "Introduction to Budget "Reconciliation," *Center on Budget and Policy Priorities*, May 6, 2022, https://www.cbpp.org/research/introduction-to-budget-reconciliation#:~:text=Congress%20sometimes%20uses%20a%20special,frequently%20asked%20questions%20about%20reconciliation.

[185] "Justices Serving on the Court 1970 – 1989," *Oregon State*

End Notes

University, Civil Rights and Liberties, accessed May 6, 2025, https://open.oregonstate.education/civilrights/back-matter/justices-1970-1989/.

[186] "Roe v. Wade and Supreme Court Abortion Cases," *Brennan Center for Justice*, see note 18.

[187] Erwin Chemerinsky, *Worse Than Nothing: The Dangerous Fallacy of Originalism* (Yale University Press, 2022).

[188] Mark Tushnet, *Taking Back the Constitution: Activist Judges and the Next Age of American Law* (Yale University Press, 2020).

[189] Ibid.

[190] "Justices Serving on the Court 1990 – 2009," *Oregon State University, Civil Rights and Liberties*, accessed May 6, 2025, https://open.oregonstate.education/civilrights/back-matter/justices-1990-2009/.

[191] Amanda Terkel, "Scalia: Women Don't Have Constitutional Protection Against Discrimination," *HuffPost*, January 3, 2011, https://www.huffpost.com/entry/scalia-women-discrimination-constitution_n_803813.

[192] "Roe v. Wade and Supreme Court Abortion Cases," *Brennan Center for Justice*, see note 18.

[193] Mark Pattison, "Survey: Majority of U.S. Catholics Oppose Overturning of Roe v. Wade," *National Catholic Reporter*, October 28, 2022, https://www.ncronline.org/news/survey-majority-us-catholics-oppose-overturning-roe-v-wade.

[194] Strine Jr. and Walter, "Originalist or Original," see note 21.

[195] Lawrence Hurley, "'Originalism is a Dead Letter': Supreme Court Accused of Abandoning Legal Principles in Trump Immunity

End Notes

Ruling," *NBC News*, July 2, 2024, https://www.nbcnews.com/politics/supreme-court/originalism-dead-letter-supreme-court-majority-accused-abandoning-lega-rcna159945.

[196] Tushnet, *Taking Back the Constitution*, see note 188.

[197] Jon Meachum, *The Soul of America: The Battle for Our Better Angels* (Random House Trade Paperbacks, 2019).

[198] "Party Divisions of the House of Representatives, 1789 to Present," *History, Art & Archives*, accessed May 6, 2025, https://history.house.gov/Institution/Party-Divisions/Party-Divisions/.

[199] "Party Division," *United States Senate*, accessed May 6, 2025, https://www.senate.gov/history/partydiv.htm.

[200] Natalie Fertig, "The People Who Brought You Bill Clinton Want to Introduce You to the 'Colorado Way'", *Politico*, July 6, 2025, https://www.politico.com/news/magazine/2025/07/06/the-colorado-way-democratic-party-00370340.

[201] "Colorado General Assembly", Balletpedia, accessed July 8, 2025, https://ballotpedia.org/Colorado_General_Assembly.

[202] Caitlin Kulperger, "Abortion Access: Women Fight Back in a Post-Dobbs Nation," *National Organization for Women*, November 4, 2024, https://now.org/blog/abortion-access-women-fight-back-in-a-post-dobbs-nation/#:~:text=Across%20the%20country%2C%20stories%20like,critical%20reproductive%20care%20in%2Dstate.

123

End Notes

[203] Adam Schrager, Bob Witwer, *The Blueprint: How the Democrats Won Colorado (and Why Republicans Everywhere Should Care)*. (Fulcrum Publishing, 2010.)

[204] Ibid.

[205] Ibid.

[206] Ibid.

[207] Fertig, The People Who Brought You Bill Clinton Want to Introduce You to the 'Colorado Way'", see note 200.

[208] Ibid.

[209] Ibid.

[210] Andrew Kenney, "Unaffiliated voters won't be blocked from open primaries in Colorado this June, judge rules," *CPR News*, February 2, 2024, https://www.cpr.org/2024/02/02/unaffiliated-voters-free-to-participate-democratic-republican-open-primaries/.

[211] Fertig, The People Who Brought You Bill Clinton Want to Introduce You to the 'Colorado Way'," see note 200.

www.ingramcontent.com/pod-product-compliance
Lightning Source LLC
Chambersburg PA
CBHW020549030426
42337CB00013B/1023